EXISTENTIAL PSYCHOTHERAPY

GARDNER PRESS SERIES
IN CLINICAL SOCIAL WORK
Edited by MARY L. GOTTESFELD

SEPARATION-INDIVIDUATION: Theory & Clinical Practice
by JOYCE EDWARD, NATHENE RUSKIN,
PATSY TURRINI

EXISTENTIAL PSYCHOTHERAPY: The Process of Caring
by DAVID G. EDWARDS

Existential Psychotherapy

The Process of Caring

DAVID G. EDWARDS, M.S.W., Ph.D.

GARDNER PRESS, INC., NEW YORK

GARDNER PRESS, INC.
19 Union Square West
New York 10003

Library of Congress Cataloging in Publication Data

Edwards, David G., 1918–
    Existential psychotherapy.

    Bibliography: p.
    Includes index.
    1. Existential psychotherapy.   2. Self-perception.
I. Title.   [DNLM: 1. Existentialism.   2. Psycho-
therapy—Methods. WM 420 E26e]
RC489.E93E38   616.89'14   81-6505
ISBN 0-89876-007-0   AACR2

Printed in the United States of America

Book Design by Sidney Solomon

CONTENTS

v

ACKNOWLEDGMENTS

The author gratefully acknowledges permission from the copyright owners to reprint excerpts from the following:

I and Thou by Martin Buber. Second edition, translated by Ronald Gregor Smith. Copyright © 1958 by Charles Scribner's Sons, New York.
The Myth of Sisyphus and Other Essays by Albert Camus. Translated by Justin O'Brien. Copyright © 1955 by Alfred A. Knopf, Inc., New York. Published by Hamish Hamilton Ltd., London.
"Rational Emotive Therapy" by Albert Ellis, Ph.D., quoted from *Current Psychotherapies*. Second Edition, edited by Ralph Corsini. Copyright © 1979 by F. E. Peacock, Publishers, Inc., Itasca, Illinois.
"What is Metaphysics?" by Martin Heidegger, from *Existence and Being*. Edited by Werner Brock. Copyright © 1949 by Regnery/Gateway, Inc., South Bend, Indiana.
The Nature of Psychotherapy by Karl Jaspers. Translated by J. Hoenig and Marian W. Hamilton. Published by Manchester University Press, 1964, and reprinted by the University of Chicago Press, Chicago. Copyright © 1964 by Karl Jaspers. Used by permission of the University of Chicago Press.
The Human Ground by Stanley Keleman. Copyright © 1975 by Stanley Keleman. Used by permission of Science and Behavior Books, Palo Alto, California.
On Shame and the Search for Identity by Helen Merrill Lynd. Copyright © 1958 by Harcourt Brace Jovanovich, Inc., New York.
"Psychodrama" by Jacob Moreno. From *Psychotherapy and Counseling*. Edited by W. Sahakian. Copyright © 1976 by Rand McNally College Publishing Company, Chicago.
Gestalt Therapy by Frederick Perls, M.D., Ph.D., Ralph

Clinical Social Work Journal, Human Sciences Press, publishers, Vol. 1, No. 1., 1973, pp. 3-12; Vol. 4, No. 1., 1976, pp. 3-13; Vol. 5, No. 2., 1977, pp. 168-173.

Journal of Contemporary Psychotherapy. Editor: Wilfred Quaytman, Ph.D. Vol. 9, No. 1, Summer 1977, pp. 89-94.

Voices: Journal of the American Academy of Psychotherapists. Vol. 13, No. 1 Spring, 1977, pp. 67-72.

Marriage and Family Counselors Quarterly. Vol. XII, No. 2, Winter 1978, pp. 32-36.

I wish to thank the following persons for their helpful criticism and discussion in the preparation of this book: Mary M. Goulding, Robert L. Goulding, Leonard Campos, John Frykman, David Hoban; Mary L. Gottesfeld, General Editor of the Gardner Press Clinical Social Work Series; Gardner M. Spungin, Publisher; the author's colleagues in the San Benito County Mental Health Services and in the Santa Clara County Mental Health Services; and, most especially, my wife, Margot E. Edwards, for her caring and encouragement.

INTRODUCTION

Of all the tasks which make up the process of psychotherapy, the communication of caring is the most important. Caring deserves this place of preeminence because the ultimate goal of therapy is to decide to live-for one*self*. Living-for one*self* is the faithful projection of one's capacities for creating trusting relationship with human partners. "Trusting relationship" implies the capacity to make free choices, to honor spontaneous creativity, and to heal one's own suffering. These are existential tasks.

The learning of caring is the most neglected aspect of a therapist's education. Many reasons can be found for this. One is the assumption that one can only attain the capacity to care by miraculous endowment. Some schools of therapy discourage the communication of caring in either direction between client and therapist in the interest of analytic objectivity. In this method of therapy nothing is real that cannot be put on the table for examination, discussion, and, in the case of the student, grading. For the author of a book on therapeutic technique, caring is an embarrassment because caring is not something to do but something to *be*. The purpose of this book is to describe the existential character of caring and to invite the reader to discover the expression of caring. It is addressed to all those who are in the process of becoming therapists.

The theme of this book is that the goals of psychotherapy are choice, spontaneity, and caring—for both client and therapist. The therapist is a behavioral model for the client. The client will find no more freedom than the therapist allows for himself. This work will expose the reader to the view that the existential reality of human be-ing demands more than mood adjustment and enhancement of coping skills. It presents the paradoxical possibility that personal liberation can only come through a passionate, spiritual commitment to another human being who is even more contradictory and more unlovable than oneself.

This book will provide direction for those seeking to explore the common existential core of some of the major therapeutic systems. This includes upper-division postgraduate students in psychiatry, psychology, social work, and counseling specialties as well as those already in the field who are seeking to enlarge their grasp of human capacity. The objectives of this work are to define the principles of existential philosophy that form the basis of therapeutic interaction between client and therapist, to describe an existential theory of personality, to illustrate applications of existential therapy, and to present a bibliography that will introduce one to an awareness of his or her own potential for authentic self-expression.

The book is a witness to the author's personal experience in pursuing these objectives. It is an expression of my conviction that the curative experience of therapy is the faithful meeting of two human beings that changes the existence of both of them. In particular it reflects my appreciation of three men whom I have known only by their writings: Albert Schweitzer, Martin Heidegger, and Soren Kierkegaard. They represent for me the possibilities for faithful expression which can be achieved by penetrating scholarship, logical thinking, and courageous self-exploration. This book is also an expression of appreciation to Bob Goulding and Jim Simkin for their indispensable help in showing me how to be a therapist.

EXISTENTIAL PSYCHOTHERAPY

I

THE HEALING
OF SUFFERING

IN PSYCHOTHERAPY
the healing of suffering is not an instrumental procedure by
which the therapist removes an offending organ or banishes a
deadly organism. Healing is accomplished by the existential
process of caring. The existential nature of caring is expressed
through language. If I say I *have* cares, I mean that I am bur-
dened by objective tasks that I possess. If I am enjoined to be
careful, I am being warned to take an existential stance. If I
am being cared *for*, I am in an existential relationship. When
I *am* caring, I have invoked a process of *self*-transcendence.

It is my thesis that the projection of transcendent *self*-
expression constitutes the essential closure of the process of
psychotherapy. Existential *self*-expression produces closure
because it surpasses the aesthetic failures and ethical deficits
of ego and its self-objects and liberates the authentic humanity of the individual. When this is accomplished, the individ-

1

ual can conclude therapy with a sense of strength and enrichment and can now negotiate the vicissitudes of living without recourse to illusions that prevent one from making empathic contact with other human beings that he or she wishes to love and care for.

The two principal illusions that paralyze *self*-transcendence are: first, that I am a very special person and therefore, invincible; and, if I am not, I *ought* to be; and, second, that I live in a nurturing and protective universe and, if it is not, it *ought* to be. Now, these two beliefs are pure illusion, and I know it. But, existentialism does not suggest that I give up these illusions which are so precious to me. It imposes the infinitely harder condition that I recognize that I alone am responsible for my belief in these illusions. I cannot blame God or Freud or anybody else. I alone have endowed these illusions with truth and power and committed my life and my belief to them. When I can own my responsibility for believing these illusions, I can cease the futile effort to impose them on an indifferent environment and live without despair, envy, and resentment. This is the existential act of *self*-transcendence called *faith*.

Existentially directed therapy also liberates the individual by transcending the need to solve the problem of moral failure as a therapeutic goal. It is not that I do not honor the moral code of society, but that I no longer need to invoke an unconscious determinism to protect me from personal responsibility. I no longer have to believe that my choices should control the world. I can only choose and take my chances on the outcome. Choice conveys a burden of uncertainty but it liberates one from immobility.

The way one regards the world is an indicator of the way one regards oneself. To the same extent that one reduces the world to an assembly of choiceless, timeless objects to be manipulated, he isolates himself from the spiritual basis of humankind. This is not said to attempt to revive support for

2

surrender of human choice to occult powers but to affirm the belief that effective therapy needs to reach the individual's transcendent *self*hood. The basis of meaningful choice that leads to transcendent *self*hood is Care. The purpose of this work is to invite one to relinquish the undoubted predictability of a linear cause-effect world and risk the uncertainties of paradoxical reality.

A prime principle of existentialism is the inseparability of paradoxical polarities such as suffering/healing, love/hate, joy/sorrow, freedom/compulsion, etc., and it follows from this that one alienates himself from *self*-support by the intellectual effort to resolve these polarities into idealistic absolutes. In a world of idealistic absolutes polar opposites are deprived of reality and explained away as the result of moral failure. In the moral world, hate is the absence of love; pain is the absence of pleasure; evil is the absence of goodness; and error is the absence of truth. Existential philosophy calls one to awake from this dream world, and, in the words of Jung, "gaze into the face of absolute evil." (Jung, 1971, p. 148)

The moral world avoids the reality of suffering and its morality justifies this avoidance. Frankl has made the understanding—not the justification—of suffering a therapeutic principle (Fabry, 1968). Simone Weil, that contradictory and perplexing saint, lived a life of self-imposed suffering. In the following passage she prophetically describes the predicament under which the client labors: the tendency of the fortunate to see catastrophe as the client's natural vocation and to ignore its effects on his soul. And Weil invokes *self*-transcendence as the movement of liberation.

The relations between destiny and the human soul, the extent to which each soul creates its own destiny, the questions of what elements in the soul are transformed by merciless necessity as it tailors the soul to fit the requirements of shifting fate, and of what elements can on the other hand be preserved, through the exercise of virtue and through grace—this whole question is fraught with

3

temptations to falsehood, temptations that are positively enhanced by pride, by shame, by hatred, contempt, indifference, by the will to oblivion or to ignorance. Moreover, nothing is so rare as to see misfortune fairly portrayed; the tendency is either to treat the unfortunate person as though catastrophe were his natural vocation, or to ignore the effects of misfortune on the soul, to assume, that is, that the soul can suffer and remain unmarked by it, can fail, in fact, to be recast in misfortune's image. . . . To define force — it is that x that turns anybody who is subjected to it into a *thing*. Exercised to the limit, it turns man into a thing in the most literal sense; it makes a corpse out of him. Somebody was there, and the next minute there is nobody here at all. . . . Here we see force in its grossest and most summary form — the force that kills. How much more varied in its processes, how much more surprising in its effects is the other force, the force that does *not* kill, i.e., that does not kill just yet. It will surely kill, it will possibly kill, or perhaps it merely hangs, poised and ready, over the head of the creature it *can* kill, at any moment, which is to say at every moment. In whatever aspect, its effect is the same: it turns a man into a stone. From its first property (the ability to turn a human being into a thing by the simple method of killing him) flows another, quite prodigious too in its way, the ability to turn a human being into a thing while he is still alive. He is alive; he has a soul; and yet — he is a thing. An extraordinary entity this — a thing that has a soul. And as for the soul, what an extraordinary house it finds itself in! Who can say what it costs it, moment by moment, to accommodate itself to this residence, how much writhing and bending, folding and pleating are required of it? It was not made to live inside a thing; if it does so, under pressure of necessity, there is not a single element of its nature to which violence is not done. . . . To be outside a situation so violent as this is to find it inconceivable; to be inside it is to be unable to conceive its end. . . . The mind ought to find a way out, but the mind has lost all capacity to so much as look outward. The mind is completely absorbed in doing itself violence. Always in human life, whether war or slavery is in question, intolerable sufferings continue, as it were, by the force of their own specific gravity, and so look to the outsider as though they were easy to bear; actually, they continue because they have deprived the sufferer of the resources which might serve to extricate him. . . . But however caused, this petrifactive quality of force, two-fold always, is essential to its nature; and a soul which has entered the province of force will not escape this except

4

by a miracle. Such miracles are rare and of brief duration. . . .

The soul that awakes then, to live for an instant only and be lost almost at once in force's vast kingdom, awakes pure and whole; it contains no ambiguities, nothing complicated or turbid; it has no room for anything but courage and love. Sometimes . . . a man finds his soul . . . as he tries to face destiny on his own terms, without the help of gods or men. At other times, it is in a moment of love that men discover their souls . . . (Simone Weil, 1956, pp. 3–5, 22, 27, 35)

Here in its monstrous reality the agency of mental disorder has been detailed by Simone Weil—the petrifactive fear that turns the body to stone and barricades the soul beyond the reach of torture. Here we see the excuses given by existential philosophers to exonerate their insensitivity to misery. Here we see the reality of that unremarkable diagnosis, "low ego-strength." For the therapist meeting with a depressed, child-beating mother, or a defiant adolescent, these lines can inspire the humility needed to touch the human *be*-ing of such a client. For the worker confronted with a dangerously violent individual in handcuffs these words can remind one that this person's desire for revenge may be the last flicker of light to guide the therapist toward a *self* encased in terrible darkness.

Society tells the individual that one is vulnerable because one is poor, sick, ugly, uneducated, crippled, deviate. And, therefore: defective; and defective equals bad. There is nothing the therapist can do to change this cultural dictum; and certainly one cannot ignore it, particularly if one is employed by the establishment that governs by it. Those who choose to forfeit the rewards offered for struggling for a place in such a society do not seek psychotherapy. Those who seek psychotherapy are those who want to compete for a place in this society but have found the cost too great for them.

5

Children can discover at an early age that social status may be gauged by sensitivity to suffering because those who are insensitive to suffering can get their way by inflicting it on those who are not. It is ironic that a society which organizes itself to protect its members from suffering imposes its will by the threat of suffering. It is understandable that a therapy founded to accommodate the casualties of this system would not think to ask the question: Why is judgment needed to justify suffering? In such a society it is foolish to believe that an answer is possible and dangerous to provide one. When it comes to recognizing therapy's mission to promote the client's valid need for rebellion, some practitioners act as if the fact that "the king has no clothes" is a secret known only by the cognoscenti while others extol nudity as a positive virtue. But neither of them are willing to challenge their complicity in the use of judgments to "explain" suffering as long as it can be rationally demonstrated "why" they suffer. And the capacity for this endurance is what they first seek from the therapist. Only when they are willing to experience *that* they suffer, does resistance stop and fear of vulnerability dissolve. When therapists become alive to the guilt and shame that conceal their own suffering — at that moment — the clients will be willing to discover their pain.

The popular testimonial approach to therapy sells books and fills workshops. However, confessions of the courage and sensitivity required to demonstrate to the client that another human has known and can hear the cry of a dying life are rarely reported and heavily disguised when they are. In a culture that prides itself on its scientific ability to maintain life after the will to live has died, human sensitivity and courage belong to the dark ages of superstitious ignorance.

Von Weizacker writes, "Only when the doctor has been deeply touched by the illness, infected by it, excited, frightened, shaken, only when it has been transferred to him, continues in him and is referred to himself by his own consciousness — only then and to that extent can he deal with it successfully." (Jaspers, 1964, p. 27)

A prime goal for existential psychotherapy is deliverance from the idea that suffering is a punishment for transgression

6

of universal judgment. Neither is suffering to be considered a road to ennobling merit. Existential therapy deals with one's reactions to what occurs in living as something that is here-now, to be lived through, and finished with. This is in conflict with cultural traditions that explain suffering as a consequence of the cosmic failures of the past and look for deliverance by salvation in the future. As a common social enterprise, psychotherapy must share the responsibility of supporting established cultural traditions. Indeed, this support arises both from the expectations which the client brings, as well as from the desire of the therapist to meet these expectations. Those who ask, Why am I suffering? What did I do to deserve this punishment? and Who can deliver me from this judgment? can hardly be expected to be ready to hear that their own vulnerability to suffering is the cancer that is secretly killing them. Scarcely more can the therapist find words to convey to clients that their capacity for sensitivity to suffering is at the same time their capacity for joy and life.

For those individuals, client and therapist, who wish to support the cultural mission of deflecting and dissipating their need for vindication, society has invented some palliative strategies. The psychotherapeutic version of these can be recognized as follows:

1) *Miracle:* A miracle is an intervention which sets aside objective cause-effect. For therapists who set store on their capacity to relieve the patient's suffering, any improvement will be a miracle.

2) *Positive Thinking:* Somebody up there likes me/my therapist likes me/I like me; and, therefore, I will get what I want. This works as long as the client agrees to want only what the therapist is willing to give.

3) *Scientific Psychiatry:* No one is responsible for scientifically discovered and invented diseases like alcoholism or schizophrenia; so clients can be grateful that their suffering can be endured without moral stigma.

4) *The New Psychology:* Repression of sexual guilt and

7

shame has now been replaced by the existential despair-of-death as a reason for suffering. No matter what the problem the client suffers from, we therapists of the new psychology deal with process, not content.

5) *Therapy as Secular Religion:* Religious orthodoxies have systematized the dispensation of judgment and forgiveness. For those who seek comfort without contrition, the secular partners of the church are there to serve.

Frankl's logotherapy (1967) sees liberation through owning the meaning of suffering. The path to this meaning includes owning the need for vindication, expressing the need for forgiveness, and expressing gratitude for the experience of liberation. The therapy meeting is the stage where these choices can be risked. The existentialist credo is that, even though we must finally bow to forces before which reason, love, and the noblest aspirations of human be-ing are meaningless absurdities, we will not surrender or appeal to irrational force. Camus has written: "Now, no one will live this fate, knowing it to be absurd, unless he does everything to keep before him that absurd(ity) brought to light by consciousness. Negating one of the terms of the opposition on which he lives amounts to escaping it." (1955, p. 40)

There is that polarity that we dare to escape, the polarity that transcends the unjust rule of gods, man, and nature, the polarity of love and death. To rational man it is absurd. To moral man it is tragic. To existential man it invites an offering of faith. This offering is that a man care for the world which will die when he does. This is the only world worth dying for.

CHAPTER

II

SHAME AND PAIN

"SHUT UP OR I'LL REAL-
ly give you something to cry about." This message from mother to child, which can be overheard almost every day in the
supermarket aisles and is probably one of the yet-to-be de-
ciphered inscriptions on the tomb of the Pharaoh, might have
been familiar to Freud in 1893 when he stated the hypothesis:
"Mortification suffered in silence" is a source of neurotic illness (Lewis, 1971, p. 392). It is important, in exploring the
contribution of shame to neurotic illness to distinguish between pain related to shame and pain related to guilt or anxiety. Here, mortification is synonomous with a painful injury
— almost a life-threatening one. The subject's silence, in spite
of the fact that oneself is suffering this painful injury, is secured by the threat of shame. Thus the mortification itself is
not shameful. Shame hides the unwillingness of the other to
respond to the victim's pain as though the pain were a fault of
the sufferer. To regard the "mortification" itself as shame-ful

is to fail to see that shame is the means by which silence is secured. In our culture, terror is used to drive one away, moral (as opposed to existential) guilt is used to make one "try harder," and shame is imposed to make one "shut up." The full import, then, of the message to shut up is that the child has the alternative of suffering the pain of the first "injury" in silence or incurring a "really" more painful and longer-lasting injury with the certainty that oneself will be helpless to avoid the rejection that will follow if one continues to seek consolation from the other. The child's realization of this defeat is the experience of shame. Thus shame is one of the child's earliest experiences in life.

Shame, if it is mentioned at all in most current texts on psychology and psychotherapy, is outnumbered by references to guilt in a ratio of five to one or greater; and guilt is correspondingly outnumbered by references to anxiety. Thus, of the three feelings — anxiety, guilt, and shame — shame would seem to have a relatively minor effect on the determination of human behavior. Dynamic psychology, as it has developed in the last 75 years, has, however, based itself on a foreshortened perspective of both natural and human world. Freud's science was based on the optimism of Newtonian mechanics, which guaranteed the ultimate knowability of nature. The scientific revolution of Planck, Einstein, Bohr, and Heisenberg was without impact on Freud. Coming from the Vienna of Strauss and Beethoven, Freud also shared the optimistic world-view that human achievement transcended national boundaries. Freud's mission was to raise man's psyche from the black ignorance of shame and magic to the light of reason and freedom demanded by a society of industrial specialization and democratic institutions. That the culture Freud wanted man to adapt to perished on the battlefields of world war, that the universe which once seemed so predictable evaporated into ultimate unknowability was no fault of Freud's. His vision of a place for human decency in a world of knowable laws was worthy of him.

The eclipse of shame as a force for social control has only occurred relatively recently, however; and, like every object in eclipse, it is still there, invisibly exercising its gravitational pull. As Lynd (1958) describes, 100 years ago, shame was easily recognizable as a vital social influence. Even 50 years ago the theme of overcoming shame generated significant interest in the popular literary market. Today, however, long-range missiles and antifertility hormones have largely isolated Western society from contact with disgraceful events; and, as the Watergate scandal demonstrated, shame as a mode of social control has exhausted much of its currency.

Kierkegaard predicted well the dilemma of a society based on industrial consumerism when he wrote: "In an age without passion, in a reflective age, intelligence has transformed daring and enthusiasm into a feat of skill. (Auden, 1952, p. 34)

As an industrial consumer economy invents calculative techniques for removing the symptoms of social problems, moral passion is abandoned as a method of dealing with these problems. Indeed, the TV channels have all too well chronicled the replacement of heroic adventure by demonic cleverness as today's route to social renown.

When psychotherapy could take heroic passion for granted as a motivation for human achievement, the intelligent application of moral guilt as an incentive for successful problem-solving was a viable therapeutic goal. Today, when the pervasive and prevailing affliction of Western humanity is the death of passion, unrecognized and unanalyzed shame is a stubborn obstacle to therapy, as Lewis (1971) has pointed out. What the new "growth" therapies seem to be saying, if their lesson be read existentially, is that resensitization to feelings of shame is a key to reviving human capacity for love; and that the traditional guilt-oriented focus of psychotherapy needs to be reevaluated. *11*

According to Bellak, Hurvich, and Gediman (1973, p. 193), Freud saw shame, disgust, and morality as reaction formations developed to avoid unpleasurable feelings triggered by childhood sexual impulses. This would be consistent with the view that improved ego-functioning would lessen the influence of primitive emotions on human behavior. Bellak's summation of ego-functioning indicates that there is minimal psychoanalytic interest in defining differences between shame and guilt. Erikson (1950) was principally responsible for inviting the examination of the social consequences of shame as distinguished from guilt and anxiety. With the naming of the maturational stages of childhood as Trust vs. Mistrust, Autonomy vs. Shame, and Initiative vs. Guilt, Erikson accorded shame a behavioral constellation in its own right. Only three other works devoting major attention to shame — Piers and Singer (1953), Lynd (1958), and Lewis (1971) — are cited by Bellak. Both Lynd and Lewis present detailed analyses differentiating shame from guilt which deserve careful study. An abbreviated table comparing shame and guilt from the perspective of social transactions is presented below.

Shame	*Guilt*
I must be the right kind of person to be acceptable.	I must prove I am acceptable.
There is no second chance.	I will be forgiven if I work hard.
I must hide my shame.	I must suffer my guilt.
Thinking is magic.	Thinking is logic.
I must be protected by friends.	I am protected by the rules of society.
There is no compromise with antagonists.	Justice will always win: Evil will be punished.
Violence is inevitable.	Negotiation is laudable.
Rewards go to the lucky.	Rewards go to the deserving.

12 This comparison demonstrates that important behavioral distinctions can be made between shame and guilt. A brief excursion into psychohistory will place shame in perspective with the global social imperatives: Submit or be anxious;

Hide or be ashamed; and Pay or be guilty. At the most primitive social level, the tribal ethic is is Submit or Be Anxious — Anxious that we will abandon you to die. In the tribe, the chief is the sole and absolute authority. The group thinks what he thinks and feels what he feels. No deviations are allowable, and when the tribal curse of death is pronounced, the victim dies forthwith. The only social advance at the tribal level was to elevate the source of authority from the local chief to an absolute religious deity. Sadly enough, this strategy of socialization is still used with young children. The mother who locks her 2-year-old in a dark closet or asks the local police to lock the children in a cell as an object lesson has not become extinct. An interesting variation of this was the parents who settled arguments among the children in the car by stopping the car, putting the 2- and 4-year-old on the steps of a large public building, which they identified as "the orphanage," and driving off for 15 minutes — which must have seemed like 15 hours to the children.

When the level of social organization went from the tribe to the nation, authority went from the chief to the absolute monarch and at this level shame became a more visible social force. Shame is a less potent social weapon than the curse of death, but the expression "I could have died of shame" betrays its ancient origins. In barbaric societies "face" is paramount. There is no remedy for dishonor — nor any forgiveness. The defective are outcasts. The social response to shame is to hide. Shame is a method of repressing expression of feelings by children. The black mother in the South, for example, insures the survival of her children by shaming them into repressing appropriate anger at white injustice. And their white antagonists are equally in the grip of shame — even when they have learned to totally deny it. Only the truly shameless can murder with impunity, let alone an author write statements like this without feeling ashamed. While nations are torturing and killing millions of their own people, no

13

slander is unthinkable. The shame ethic represses anger and forecasts the eruption of explosive violence. The mode of thinking congruent with the shame ethic is magic thinking. Good is unchallengeable and evil is proscribed. Success is guaranteed by the right toothpaste or the right ideology — logic is superfluous. Magic thinking is the touchstone of the politics of shame. Be it master race or silent majority, to doubt the evil intentions of the enemy is equivalent to inviting him to rape your wife.

Civilization rises from the level of shame and magic to the level of guilt and responsibility. Theoretically, civilization operates by logic, negotiation, and compromise. The guilt ethic says that you are not defective, you only need to try harder; and it supplies the rules for calculating the values, standards, and penalties governing civilized behavior. The expectation of rehabilitation is based on guilt, not shame. The history of Western religious dogma records these stages of socialization. First, the tribal god Jehovah holds unquestioned dominion over the lives of the chosen. Second, the epic of the atonement removes the burden of original shame (sin). And, finally, Dostoevsky's "Cardinal" encounters Jesus and tells Him that man prefers the guilt ethic of the church to spiritual liberation. Just as an individual who has negotiated Erikson's three maturational tasks never completely finishes with any of them, so is society interpenetrated at its highest levels with residues from its barbaric and primitive stages. Just as individuals regress under stress, so does society. When control based on guilt fails, regression, first to shame and then to violence occurs. At the level of organized violence it is obvious that the guilt ethic is not working. What is more fateful for civilized society is its failure to recognize that a resort to the shame ethic precludes the success of institutions based on the guilt ethic. Notably, the social welfare and penal systems are established to rehabilitate according to the guilt ethic. When, however, they are administered according to the shame ethic, the message is clear — "You are irredeemable."

14

A goal of psychotherapy is to liberate the individual from the burden of these social imperatives so that one can adapt without being handicapped, love without hiding, and work without suffering. The penalty for adopting these cultural strategies in dealing with anxiety, shame, and guilt is that in achieving security from anxiety, the individual denies the inevitability of death; in achieving release from shame, one forfeits the curative use of anger; and by accepting cultural guarantees of protection from guilt, one loses the possibility of liberation. It has remained for existential psychotherapy to forcefully make the point that adaptation to cultural norms and personal survival are by no means synonomous. Existential psychotherapy sees feelings of anxiety, shame, and guilt as primary agents urgently signaling a threat to survival and claiming a hearing in their own right instead of being signs pointing to an elusive internal conflict that invites insightful exploration and discovery.

The irresolvable dilemma which the individual faces, and which psychotherapy cannot adjust, is the prospect that the Other one engages with will turn out to be both a healing ally and a deadly adversary. In the contest for survival, the individual learns to solve problems caused by conflicts between the demands of the environment and biological needs and psychic wants. Pain arises at the prospect of failure of problem-solving efforts. Anxiety is not fear of unknown danger but fear of the real danger which the individual is powerless to defend against—abandonment to death, as Kierkegaard has convincingly stated (1941 b). Fear of abandonment and the shame of defeat are the earliest traumatic experiences of humans. Fear of social exclusion as well as fear of being penalized for failure are reinforced by a culture of competitive individualism. Admittedly, one of the functions of the therapeutic process is to train the client to discriminate between and respond differentially to threats that are immediately present as compared to reactivated memories of past traumas. However, any process that diminishes the individual's sensitivity to pain is countertherapeutic and reinforces neurotic immobilization. The formula for neurotic capitulation is: Better dead than hurting—hurting from being abandoned, humiliated, and punished. Depression is existential mourning for this death of the drive for survival. A civilized variation of this is: Better guilty than humiliated, as Lynd points out.

Acknowledgment of personal sin or confession of guilt may sometimes be a defense against the possibility that there may be no meaning in the world. After some experiences of shame and fear of emptiness we may welcome guilt as a friend. Sin, guilt, punishment —each is, in one sense, an affirmation of order and significance. Shame questions the reality of any significance. Guilt in oneself is easier to face than lack of meaning in life. (1958, p. 58)

Existential therapy goes further to say that power, capacity, personal identity never can reside in the protective spell of an institutional incantation against guilt (however logical, rational or well documented by authority), but only in a passionate commitment to caring concern. Knowing in advance the inevitability of being vulnerable to abandonment, humiliation, and guilt, the individual is able to experience them fully and still ask for and show caring concern to the other. This is the never-ending process of living. To stop the process is to die emotionally. Eulogizing the deceased is a betrayal of psychotherapy.

Existential therapy moves against defenses rather than analyzing or observing them. Successful movement against defenses results in manifesting the painful feelings the defenses were developed to avoid. Dynamic therapy has largely demonstrated its skill and concern with uncovering guilt rather than shame. Experiential therapy places a great deal of emphasis on desensitizing individuals to shameful experiences but it contributes little to a basis for understanding such activity. It is my opinion that the realization of potency that

16

follows from the capacity to respond sensitively to shame is a curative experience of psychotherapy.

A brief case history will illustrate this.

A 22-year-old single woman has broken away from her recently divorced parents. She is the eldest of three children who never felt accepted by an alcoholic father. She currently feels trapped in a dead-end adolescent romance with a nonresponsive man. She says she is frustrated as she "waits" for him to make up his mind about staying with her. An exploration of her feelings of frustrated anger connected with waiting develops that she is waiting until she gets angry "enough" to tell him goodbye. Her childhood training to use shame to desensitize her to feeling pain is now immobilizing her. As she is beginning to see her ability to recognize and feel pain as belonging to her capacity for healing rather than something shameful that must be denied, her anger becomes a source of potency rather than a liability to be borne.

Shame is the social weapon by which the individual is trained to deny pain and to see his capacity to feel pain as a personal defect. The courageous use of anger is the effective counter to a shame which forbids the expression of loving concern.

Just as moral guilt is a cop-out to avoid being responsible for making decisions, shame is a cop-out to avoid being responsible for recognizing and expressing feelings. Many current systems of therapy, while according feelings an important role in the determination of behavior, overemphasize guilt because guilt is ego's motivation to solve problems. A therapy which focuses on recognition and expression of feelings will emphasize shame because shame is ego's motivation to hide feelings. An exclusive preoccupation with either decisions or feelings is a one-sided and inadequate approach to human functioning.

17

Recognition of the inhibiting power of shame is the key that opens the door to the pain of impotent rage. A recent newspaper feature headline illustrates this.

Fearful Parents Hire Detectives to Probe Drug Scene

They do not have any guilt feelings about having someone follow their children around. They only want to help before it is too late.

The parents' fear is that their children will abandon them. The parents do have guilt feelings about having detectives spy on their children; the guilt that makes them feel omnipotent enough to hire detectives originates from their anticipated shame of being exposed as failures as parents. Instead of recognizing their shame and confronting their children with their pain, they put the responsibility for their rage on the children; and when public exposure occurs, their response is inevitable: "We did all we could to save them, but they wouldn't listen."

Where avoidance of pain plays a basic part in the origination and maintenance of psychopathology, it is highly probable that shame, not guilt, is the defense that is blocking therapy. Defensive use of shame can frequently be differentiated by the characteristics of

1) fear of exposing exaggerated "defects"

2) fatalistic approach to achievement

3) belief in magical protection

4) excessive insensitivity to and denial of pain and risk of pain — "machismo"

5) excessive sensitivity to cultural taboos — especially prudery

6) aimless life-pattern

7) unwillingness to share feelings as a basis of personal relationship

When a client can be persuaded to abandon shame as a defense against the pain underlying this symptomatology, therapy can proceed.

III

HELPLESSNESS

A CRUCIAL ISSUE IN
therapy is to distinguish between the structure and content of
pathology and the process that allows the pathology to go on
being developed and produced. Clients are more than willing
to report the content of their pathology and the structure of
their defenses. What they resist recognizing, in fact undergo
great pain to conceal, is the way they disable themselves so they
can be "helped"; since only when one is helpless can one be
omnipotent enough to withstand abandonment. Thus helplessness is a defense against abandonment as shame is a defense
against anger. The therapeutic questions to pursue therefore
are: Who is going to abandon you if you don't "try harder"?;
and, Who is going to hurt you if you express rage? These are
two different issues that need to be kept separate in a therapeutic plan. Confusion of these issues is a cause of "failures" in
therapy.

Two areas in which recent recognition of the need for this

differentiation have produced results are death and suicide and addictions.

Death and Suicide

As Menninger's classic work, *Man Against Himself* (1938), points out, shame, guilt, and anxiety all play a part in predisposing a person to suicide. In the case of studies of suicide "clinics," however, shameful helplessness is rarely considered as an important motive. Nor in Kübler-Ross's (1969) analyses of the psychology of dying is helplessness prominently mentioned. Yet it is obvious that society considers death and disease as shameful defects that must be euphemistically disguised. The secret of Kübler-Ross's success in dealing with her dying patients is her ability to surrender all resistance to experiencing the desperate helplessness that dying imposes on the victim and the helper. Goulding's (1979) insistence on getting to "no-suicide" contracts with therapy patients is solidly founded on the necessity for dealing with the client's unendurable feelings of helplessness.

Shame is most critically related to incurable disease because: 1) It is a noxious social defect 2) It is irreparable — there is no forgiveness, and 3) The victims are completely helpless to justify their condition. In the face of the real or imagined prospect of this situation, suicide is the most powerful affirmation of defiance, and acceptance is the most charitable affirmation of humanity that a person can make.

20 Addictions

It is recognized that conditions such as poor impulse control, compulsive need for gratification, low-stimulus barrier, aggravated response to fear and anxiety, and failure to neutralize anxiety by defensive processes are associated with deviant and sociopathic behavior. The question seldom asked, however, is: What affect is being ignored that is urgently signaling a survival threat? When it appears that the purpose of the deviant behavior is to hide rather than to flee or confront, then the critical problem is helplessness. Whatever the compulsion for which one cannot tolerate interference, wanting to be absolved of guilt is not the addict's problem. Though one pleads passionately to be able to feel guilty, oneself cannot be guilty. One cannot "mend one's ways" because one must maintain the addiction to conceal unendurable helplessness. Any interference with the addiction threatens to reveal one's helplessness and is therefore a threat to abandonment. The basis of treatment by both Alcoholics Anonymous and Synanon is to teach the addict that one can defy helplessness without being abandoned.

Seligman (1979) points out that the expectation of being able to control the environment promotes mastery and competence while the assumption that one is doomed by an internal defect leads to helplessness. As an example of this, he cites two classroom situations: In the first situation the student is disciplined for misbehavior. In this instance the situation is time-limited, it is specific to the student's behavior, and it is attributed to the environmental situation; that is, the student believes that the conflict with the teacher will stop when he changes his behavior and he can forget about the teacher when he leaves the classroom. In the second situation the student does not present a behavior problem as a *cause* for poor academic performance so it is attributed to a personal defect —stupidity. This confirms the student's belief that he will always be helpless. In the first situation the student attributes his poor performance to prejudice on the part of the teacher. He does not think he is stupid and maintains a defiant attitude as a defense against helplessness. In the second case the

21

student believes his situation is hopeless and refuses to make an effort to do his schoolwork. Both students fail but for different reasons.

It has been found that depressed persons have a much more realistic perception of their situation than nondepressed persons. The nondepressed persons are not necessarily high achievers. Their good spirits arise by virtue of their being strongly defended against threats of failure.

There is a difference between depression and helplessness and hopelessness. The depressed person may be struggling unnecessarily with a difficult task but he knows he can stop if he wants to. The hopeless person sees himself as a permanent victim of a defect he cannot conquer or be rid of. Yet he really has not given up waiting for magic rescue and he is angry with the universe for not providing it.

White (1959) believes the drive for mastery and control supercedes "biological" drives. This would account for the insistence by clients that they must *know* why they are afflicted with their emotional disturbance. They profess to believe that this knowledge will allow them to master their "problem." They have, of course, consulted many doctors, therapists, and friends and received many professional opinions and much helpful advice to no avail. By this time they have maneuvered themselves into the position that if all these opinions are correct, they must be wrong. But to admit this would be to give up their mastery, so they are condemned to fail either way. With this realization in mind they dedicate themselves to making failures out of all their helpers. This is their *cause* of hopelessness.

Seligman states (1975, p. 105) that "the central goal of therapy for depression is the patient's regaining his belief that he can control events that are important to him." Existential philosophy proposes that the path to the relief of depression is to let go of the belief that one *must* be able to control every event that is important to one. Indeed, the experience of prisoners in concentration camps is that those who survived were able to detach themselves from their powerlessness and transcend their suffering (Frankl, 1963). Surrendering to one's powerlessness is quite a different choice than identifying with the aggressor. In the first case the individual makes his own choice and validates his own-*self*. In the second case one relinquishes the power of choice to the prison guard and forfeits *self*hood. The ones who suffer early death are those who outwardly identify with the aggressor but inwardly "hope" for magic rescue. The critical issue for the therapist is to present to the client the *reality* of emotional and material support and disabuse him of the "hope" of magic.

The lethal defect that destroys *self*hood is the conviction that one is powerless to choose one's feelings. Hope is the sense that one will maintain *self*-integrity in spite of unpredictable future events. It means that one has given up self-imposed demands for infallible control over the world. Acceptance of one's own limits of power is *self*-detachment. One does not have the power to undo the past. The business of the past only needs finishing. Hope knows how to say goodbye. For *self*-transcendence, separation is not a loss. Along with hope and *self*-transcendence goes autonomous choice. Choice makes feelings real.

The following is an example of the treatment of helplessness.

Esther is a middle-aged single mother with three children. The oldest child, 15, had a disturbed childhood prior to the parents' divorce. He has recovered considerably in the last five years but still presents behavior problems at home. Under extreme stress with him, Esther alternates between screaming and sobbing, re-enacting her past scenes with her disturbed husband. In therapy she is passive and helpless. The therapist's suggestions are typically rejected with the statement, "I've tried that and it didn't work." Esther presents a classic case of learned helplessness. In one session she relates the following dream.

23

"I am an espionage agent carrying a secret message. I go into this auditorium filled with enemies waiting for a revolutionary

speaker to appear. I am careful to look innocent but I am afraid they suspect me so I go to the restroom and throw the message in the toilet bowl. I leave without flushing the toilet and as soon as I am outside I realize that the message will be discovered and traced to me. I stand outside panic stricken and a woman goes in and flushes the toilet. As she comes out she gives me a knowing look and a wink that says everything is taken care of."

Esther worked on this dream in Gestalt fashion where she took the part of each element of the dream. As the auditorium, she is always all booked up but she doesn't have any choice over who's in her. She doesn't like some of the opinions she has to listen to but her owner is only interested in making money. As a member of the audience she is anticipating a stirring speech which will arouse her enthusiasm. She is not as interested in party goals as she is in the enthusiastic "high" she gets from hearing the speeches. As the message in the toilet, she is useless and wasted. No one will ever know her secret. As the other agent who flushes the toilet she is wise and protective of Esther. She has poise and presence that Esther envies. As herself Esther is outwardly trying to maintain a bold front as she fights for control over her anxiety and insecurity.

The dream graphically depicts the realities of Esther's life situation. The therapist made no interpretations, however. Instead he asked her if she would be willing to enter a relaxed state and participate in a guided fantasy in which she would get better-acquainted with her secret helper. In this fantasy she visualized her secret helper handling a situation that presented a pattern of stress and failure. She then made a mental "movie tape" of the helper solving the problem and stored it for use in the next stress situation. She was told that she could contact her helper by repeating the simple relaxation procedure and just watch the helper carry out the preprogrammed plans. Esther's secret helper is her intuitive preconscious self. As she learns more and more to mobilize selfhood and her sense of hopelessness diminishes, stressful situations at home will be less anxiety-provoking.

24

IV

CHOOSING FREEDOM

"I AM OLD NOW AND I
want to remember everything that was there for me once"
(Hellman, 1973). These words begin the story of a friendship
told in the motion picture, *Julia*. Symbolic of the inexorable
force of destiny, the main action of the play takes place on a
train from Paris to Berlin. The protagonist has taken this
train in order to smuggle $50,000 to her friend in the anti-
Nazi underground. As the picture opens she remembers the
train leaving the station. The picture contrasts the choiceful
freedom of one who follows the call of conscience and the pur-
poselessness of those controlled by everyday existence. The
audience is not privy to the internal conflicts of Julia, and, to
a generation who did not live through the march of dictator-
ship across Europe, she may appear to be only a sacrificial
heroine from a faraway time. The protagonist, Lilly, however, portrays the life-situation of one who is struggling to

deal with the consequences of her choice to be faithful to a loyalty that no one around her understands. That is the meaning of existential choice.

For me to-be[1] human means to know that I am responsible for the choices that I make and for the choices that I refuse to make. To have this knowledge means that I judge my self. In this process of judging my self I discover and invent arbitrary rules and authorities. These rules and authorities constitute an existential world — my world. There are three major classes of rules for forming a world: rational, moral, and existential. I can choose or refuse to-be in each of these. Thus my world always consists of a mixture of rationality, morality, and freedom. The rational world is fully determined. The axioms of nature are unbreakable and unchallengeable. A rational world is constituted from time-independent facts. If I fail to make a correct prediction I know it is merely because I have failed to properly compute the terms of the established formula or that the correct formula is yet to be discovered although it is surely there in nature's choiceless workings. In a world ruled by cause-effect I am preserved from value conflicts by a detached objectivity and the infallible operation of self-interest. The moral world is likewise determined by formulas — formulas imposed by authorities: gods, kings, churches, legislatures, parents, spouses, families, teachers, doctors, bosses, therapists, etc. My choice is simply to conform or be rejected. The moral world is constituted from eternal verities. There will always be only one correct answer. In the words of an ancient inscription: "Peace to him who does what is good and death to him who does not."

To-be in an existential world means that human be-ing can never be-long to a self that thinks the meaning of its behavior is determined by an agent beyond its awareness. To defend against an emotion is to avoid being aware of a *self* that could feel that emotion. But I know that *self* exists, therefore, I must dread the discovery of that self. Aware *self* is not just the individual who fears but a *self* that fears to be aware of that fear. Otherwise there would be no fear. A discussion of height phobia will illustrate this. I become irrationally anxious and violently ill because I fear to look over the edge of a tall building. I get sick just thinking about it. I can give no rational reason why the simple thought of looking over the edge of a tall building should make me sick when I am sitting in my therapist's office on the ground floor of a one-story building. Obviously, I have repressed the real object of my fear into my unconscious. Dynamic psychology will explain to me how my unconscious holds this power over me. Existential psychotherapy does not deny the power of unconscious repression. In fact, it has so much respect for it that it is not willing to attempt to force or trick the unconscious into revealing its dreadful secret.

Existential therapy asks, What possibility presents itself to my consciousness, when I think of looking over the edge of a tall building, that is so dreadful that I must resist the thought to the point of making myself physically ill? As I visualize myself shrinking up against the farthest wall from the edge, my most urgent wish is to avoid falling off. My repressed unconscious holds a multitude of messages about not killing myself; but which one is supporting my pathology? "Oh, if I could only be free of this burdensome mystery," ego says. But the immediate possibility of freedom that presents itself to my consciousness is to throw myself off the edge. Logic, however, tells me that this would kill me, so I am in conflict. How have I contrived to believe that the only way to be free is to destroy my-*self* so that it will no longer be able to know freedom. Anxiety makes my-*self* aware that I am still alive. That is the threat — to be alive in a world that denies to me the actuality to-be free. But that is where I am mistaken. It is not the actuality of my world that allows me the possibility to-be free. It is my-*self*. My phobic symptoms are not unconsciously determined. On the contrary they are consciously enacted to reveal

27

to me the danger of the possibility that I might destroy my-*self*. Repression operates to make the world plausible to ego. The unconscious would have no power over my-*self* if I did not know the difference. That is the existential world: a world beyond the reach of external authority, a world of temporal flux and tension between paradoxical opposites, and a world in which I am called by conscience to-be free. My defeat comes from rejecting this awareness.

The goal of every method of psychotherapy is to liberate the client from the choiceless, redundant situation in which he is enmeshed. There is no unitary theory of therapy, however, and each system of therapy suffers from its own self-imposed limitations on reality. I particularly want to distinguish between therapies whose end result is self-surrender to a universal absolutism and those whose goal is *self*-conscious choice of commitment to individual human beings. Erhard's e.s.t. is an example of self-surrender to absolutism. This type of self-surrender produces blissful peak experiences, to be sure, but it lacks the dimension of social responsibility necessary to make freedom meaningful.

For the last 300 years Western thinking has been engrossed with the choiceless, valueless, timeless, linear cause/effect scientific world of Cartesian dualistic logic. One reason, of course, is our dependence on the profusion of consumer comforts which science has dispensed from its cornucopia. Another is that, functionally, our trust in science is no different from the absolute loyalty which was invested in choiceless religious authority. We only discovered that God had died when the atom proved to be more reliable, but the bases for this eventuality were laid long before, in our fundamental assumptions about the nature of mass, energy, space, and time.

28   Our present firmly held convictions concerning the conservation of mass-energy, space, and time which are now so "axiomatically self-evident" were not always believed to be true (Koyre, 1958). Yet today these assumptions are the

standard by which all "truth" is ultimately judged. Truths, by which social behavior is predicted, are believed to be time-independent facts. Many current concepts about the functioning of the human mind are postulated on the basis of mythical fixed reference points modeled on the deterministic view of the universe. This view originated with Newton and terminated with Einstein who pointed out that time-independent facts exist only for an observer traveling at the speed of light. And at this speed the observer would see the whole universe shrunken to a singular point of eternally frozen immobility (Bronowski, 1973). Obviously time does not stand still for human beings on earth. We project the time-independent "real" world on the basis of a series of stop-action photographs which we have arranged to form what appears to us to be a reasonable pattern (Le Shan, 1974). Our judgment as to what a reasonable pattern is does not come from any superior intelligence somewhere out there, but is an historical product of our own laborious invention — a labor undertaken in order to deny the fatality of chaos. Yet this fatality is precisely what Sartre stated to be constitutive of pure consciousness (1957, p. 101).

Man has historically founded his ideas of value and reality on the basis of the ways he organized the patterns of his experience. As these patterns become historically accepted, they progressively begin to limit creative choice; and man's existential task becomes that of breaking out of his self-imposed limitations. Justification for accepting these limitations is claimed to be derived from transcendent authority. Religious communities accept choiceless existence in obedience to divine fiat; anarchists are content to lapse into choiceless chaos because it feels "right"; Marxists subordinate the need for choice to the locomotive of history; and the beneficiaries of scientific industrial consumerism surrender their initiative to the objective rule of scientific experiment. Surrender of initiative to transcendent authority, whether it be God, nature, or

29

the therapist means the atrophy of personal values and personal entrapment in frustrating futility. The function of the therapist is to invite the client to join in breaking out of the redundant system in which they themselves consent to become mutually engaged: the attempt to "cure" the client.

Real choice is made between an obvious polarity that arises uniquely out of intuitive experience. The illusion of choice, which demands that one make a selection from a series of pre-formulated alternatives, denies the validity of intuitive experience, and has no curative potential. For a therapy based on the client's self-determination, the issue is not to take sides in the philosophical debate of free will vs. determinism. It is to answer whether the client is to choose only between predetermined alternatives presented by others or whether it is possible to make autonomous choices based on intuitive experience. The issue of self-determination is not whether a human being can escape the fate of history or overturn the order of the universe but whether the *self* of intuitive experience can choose to discover a meaning that transcends its objectively defined world. This is the *self*-identity that existential therapists commit themselves to discovering and sharing.

CHAPTER

V

CARING CONTACT

WHAT IS CALLED "MEN-
tal illness" is the effort to deny pain and isolate one's self from
arbitrary irrationality. The symptoms resulting from the success of this effort are not illness but a survival strategy. The
task of therapy is twofold: to make caring contact with the
client and to let him know that his need for *self*-validation is
responded to.

Dynamic psychology (Freudian) defines "mental illness"
as alienation of ego from reason and logic and it devotes itself
to restoring ego-rationality. Existential therapy believes that
the emptiness that one defends against can be remedied by
the restoration of *self*-awareness. This is not the psychological
self of ego-object images such as: my house, my job, my wife,
and my feelings (i.e., my ego-opinions about object images
which produce feelings of joy, sorrow, elation, depression,
anger, etc.)

Existential therapy does not define health as a repetition of good feelings or the development of better cognitive control. It sees existence as faithful *self*-projection to make contact with the environment. The authentic expression of *self* is Caring that is shared with another human person. The projection of Caring does not draw on any psychic reservoir of Caring. It is newly created and revealed in *each* manifestation of Caring. The expression of Caring comes from *self*-awareness that trusts its own perceptions and does not serve an egologic that is the infallible judge of its own projects. Thus, *self* is neither a mental content concealed in the black box of the unconscious nor is it an instinctual energy waiting to be discharged. It is the unique manifestation of a commitment to spiritual communion encompassing the Be-ing of two individuals. To share my recognition that I have been loved and am able to accept that love is the transforming experience of therapy—for the client and the therapist.

Hate is the response to a situation in which an individual believes that love owed to him has been denied. The denial of expected love or the rejection of proffered love initiates a cyclic course of humiliation, anger, resentment, and attack. Whether the attack is expressed overtly or covertly, the individual presents himself as unloving and unlovable, thereby inviting a fresh cycle of rejection, humiliation, anger, and resentment. As this cycle is repeated over and over again, the individual becomes embedded in powerlessness and depression. From his position of helplessness, the individual denies his hostility and projects it onto others in his environment. The curative task is to break out of this self-perpetuating cycle.

The basis of this cycle is the "bad" ego-image which the person has incorporated and which ego-logic tells him he must eliminate by the defenses of denial and projection. Ego-logic tells him that the consequences of accepting the "bad" image as truly identifying him would be injurious if not fatal. The prospect of injury generates the fear that fears to be aware of itself. Thus ego barricades *self* beyond the reach of help, i.e., neurotic withdrawal.

According to ego psychology, cure is achieved by liberating ego from its attachment to its "bad" image and substituting attachment to a "good" image (object). The existential objection to this practice is that ego secretly knows that both the "good" and "bad" images are its own creation. Existentialism postulates that all attachment to ego-images is an unreal dream and when ego awakes from its dream to the reality of its loss of *self* the feelings of betrayal, anger, and fear return unabated and are indeed reinforced by the recognition of another failure. The outward evidence of this process is an attenuation of affect and a monolithic rigidity of thinking which the individual adopts as "evidence" of liberation. The joy that this person professes is an illusion that is only maintained by insulation from the reality of his life — an illusion which evaporates in the face of death. As long as ego can avoid the reality of death it is free of fear and anxiety, but when ego calls on *self* for support and receives no response its anguish is unbounded.

Existential therapy is founded on the principle that ego will be liberated from fear, anger, and despair when it gives up the fruitless search for satisfying self-objects and awakes to *self*-reality. The pathway to discovery of *self* has traditionally been the province of religion, but, whether one attributes authorship of *self* to God or to human nature, existential writers are in agreement that love is the product of *self*-awakening. Sartre described *self*-awakening as follows:

At this level man has the impression of ceaselessly escaping from himself, of overflowing himself, of being surprised by riches which are always unexpected — Perhaps not without the ego, yet as escaping from the ego on all sides, as dominating the ego and maintaining the ego outside the consciousness by continued creation. On this level, there is no distinction between the possible and the real since the appearance is the absolute. There are no more barriers, no

33

more limits, nothing to hide consciousness from *itself*. Then, consciousness noting . . . the fatality of its spontaneity, is suddenly anguished: it is this dread, absolute and without remedy, this fear of itself, which seems to us *constitutive of pure consciousness*. (Author's italics) (1957, p. 99, 101)

An essential condition for caring contact is equality of responsibility between client and therapist. Taft has written:

> The client, in our belief, is not a sick person whose illness must first be classified, but a human being, like the worker, asking for a specific service. He, no less than any other human being, finds it painful to put out a need that he can no longer meet independently, and subject his will, however feeble, to the possibility of unwelcome control in obtaining what he seeks. (Robinson, 1962, p. 269)

David Hoban reports that one client verbalized to the therapist: "If you were really going to help me, you would have to be invisible so that I would not be blinded by gratitude."

The word "gratitude" seems incongruous except in consonance with the recognition that the gratitude is for release from humiliation by authority. Brandon (1976) describes vividly the impact of the shame of helplessness shared by the client and the social worker involved in situations of need and the humiliation that awaits the worker who must compulsively present himself as "Mr. Nice Guy."

To discern the client's unspoken need is the special talent of the healer. Not in any sense an analytic mind-reader, the worker's skill is to be alert for the need which the client avoids expressing. Weiss (1975) states that, in order for this kind of revelation to occur, the client-worker relationship must transcend the level of *I-It* transactions as well as moral judgments of what "ought-to-be."

Contact with another is constituted by the flow of attention — making, breaking, and renewing contact. One is not aware of flow of attention until it stops. The stoppage occurs when one leaves the now-present. The feeling which arises is boredom. Brandon (p. 70) describes "helping" as the market-place for those who want to be in any other time and place except the present one. Krill (1978) sees therapist boredom as self-inflicted. Perls diagnoses therapist boredom as an avoidance of the figure of interest that is presenting itself. The figure of interest that the therapist wants to avoid affirming is the client's craziness and resistance. When the therapist finds himself afraid to make contact with the client, he needs to do two things: deal with his own anxiety and project a less threatening figure of interest that he and the client can attend to. One possibility is for the therapist to present his responsibility for his own anxiety as his most immediate concern.

Revelation of feeling is a frequently misunderstood facet of practice. Unconditional positive regard for the client does not mean unconditional disregard of the therapist's feelings for the client. Therapy is not a game to con the client into ignoring his bad feelings. Nor is it an opportunity for the therapist to match his own craziness with the client's. Spontaneity cannot be programmed nor can its expression be revoked. The existential therapist is a model of self-trust. I once asked a client to imagine wearing a sign that said: "I do not have to have your approval, damn you. And I like you anyway." For me, that defines positive regard. The extent to which I can truly share the client's ecstasy or suffering is measured by the extent to which I share mine with him. Brandon cites several case examples illustrating this. For workers who may be less heroic than Brandon, Weiss's case examples are equally illuminating.

The existential therapist does not operate from a position of neutral protection. He affirms the intention—indeed the will—to help. Taft states (p. 278):

Even if one [were to be] without [this] will . . . the client would put upon the most passive helper his own need to be opposed, to have someone upon whom to project the conflict which he cannot solve alone. . . . Could anything be harder than to be left so free?

[There is no procedure which] has removed from the helper the burden of responsibility for helping, without which he has no reason for existing.

In the interplay of opposition, conflict, and resolution between client and therapist, both learn to own success and failure, and compromise and vindication, as life-affirming experiences.

In his book *How Real is Real?* Watzlawick (1976) relates the considerations involved in inventing a radio message that could be understood by an intelligence 10,000 light years distant from our solar system. How we can maximize the probability that this intelligence will understand our message, is indeed a necessary consideration; but the more important question is: How can we let the recipient know 10,000 years after our death we sent the message in the certainty, that it would be recognized that we knew in advance that we would be transcendently understood? And if it be our fate, to paraphrase Unamuno (1954), that this vindication is to be denied us, let us so live as to shame that fate. The skill of the therapist lies in the ability to implant messages with the client that are yet to be understood by the client. Yet when they are eventually heard and understood, they convey the unshakable conviction to the client that the therapist understood his need and responded uniquely to him. This is transcendent communication.

VI

EXISTENTIAL
PERSONALITY THEORY

THEORIES OF PERSON-
ality are necessarily developmental. They chronicle an individual's maturational journey toward the goal of human possibility. This goal is always only a possibility because life is
open-ended. Until the moment of death, change is always
possible. Existential therapy is a theory of how choice realizes
possibility. We have talked of the experiences of suffering,
freedom, caring, shame, and helplessness and of the kinds of
rules — rational, moral, and existential — that society devises
to organize experience. Freud organized experience around
the conflict between instinctual drives and moral control.
Jung classified experience according to polarities — thinking:
feeling, sensation:intuition, introversion:extroversion.
Kohut has organized experience around nuclear ambitions
and ideals. Berne's polarity consists of Parent and Child with
Adult as a fulcrum. Perls claimed that Gestalt therapy did not
depend on arbitrary rules for support but rested on experi-

ence alone. He dealt with experiences, such as awareness, responsibility, and spontaneity. Freud pictured the life function as the discharge of tension to maintain organismic equilibrium. Jung proposed the integration of polarities to achieve individuation. Existential therapy envisions the transformation of anxiety to spontaneity and the transcendence of moral ambiguity by a "leap of faith."

Personality — persona — is the product of language and logic. It is the mask of *self*. Behind the mask, the be-ing of every person exists. What does "be-ing" mean? Be-ing is the word for that no-thing which cannot be represented by any other. Be-ing is not a property that can be added on to an object at hand, such as, "the sky is blue." Be-ing is the *is* which makes possible the process of thinking sky and blue. My *self* is the process of be-ing *me,* as in the familiar saying: Be your *self*. In the process of be-ing *me* I have (possess) psychic images (objects) but I am *in* dread, despair, love, ecstasy. I *am* guilty, ashamed, penitent. These are existential processes, not psychic objects. The existential process only occurs in the *presence* of another human being from whom I seek a caring response. In this moment of contact the vision of change is revealed.

Existential process is the process of being-toward-the-future. Not that I *have* a future to live out that is inexorably predetermined, but one that is yet-to-happen depending on the choices that *I* make. The enterprise of existential psychotherapy is to liberate *self*-awareness that *I* can make choices that change my own future. The identity which continually emerges in moments-of-vision defines its *self* in the process of emerging. Existential therapy is the study of the structure of be-ing that makes this process possible. This structure is called faith.

38

Soren Kierkegaard (1813-1855) was the prophet of existential faith. Kierkegaard's work was published in Danish and not widely read in Europe before 1900 or in English before

1930. While existential therapy has only had an audience in America since 1960, it has been recognized in Europe since 1920.[2] Karl Jaspers (1883-1969), a psychiatrist and an existential philosopher, was a contemporary of Freud and his book *General Psychopathology*, originally published in 1913, has appeared subsequently in seven editions. *Existence* published by May, Angel, and Ellenberger in 1958 was a pioneer English presentation of the principles and practice of existential psychotherapy. Victor Frankl, a Viennese therapist, is a leading spokesman for existential therapy.[3] Since 1959 he has been publishing in English. His book *Psychotherapy and Existentialism* (1967) presents an excellent review of the position of existential psychotherapy with relation to psychodynamic and humanistic therapies. Frankl's principles, especially paradoxical intention and dereflection, have been widely adopted by today's experiential and systems therapies. The most important book since *Existence* has just been published by Yalom (1980). His book *Existential Psychotherapy* is an impressive discussion of the field which is not likely to be equalled in the next 25 years.

Kierkegaard laid the foundation of existential psychotherapy. He described the structure of existential being and the process for the discovery of transcendent *self*hood. Existential psychotherapy has no new techniques of therapy to propose, but it is exciting news that what Kierkegaard predicted 150 years ago has been confirmed by the work of Kohut. Kierkegaard stated that individuals are in despair until they find a commitment that gives their life a serious meaning. In the attempt to choose a life-purpose, individuals are confronted with paradoxical options and their life task is to justify their choices. Every appeal to an authority short of transcendent *self*hood leads to despair. Indeed, despair is the means by which *self*hood makes this denial known. To compromise in despair is the betrayal of personal destiny. Kierkegaard defines five possible conditions of life-purpose:

1) No relevant commitment (purposeless living).

2) Use of natural skills (aesthetic living).

3) Social duty (ethical living).

4) Discovery of *self*-identity that is not derived from aesthetic or ethical experience (universal transcendence, nonattachment in the Eastern sense).

5) Discovery of *self*-identity which owes its existence to a relationship that paradoxically redeems the meaning of aesthetic and ethical experience (the leap of faith).

For Kierkegaard the aesthetic life was living for the excitement of immediate sensation. Aesthetic enjoyment could be derived from contemplating works of art, from the performance of feats of athletic skill, from the thrill of scientific discovery, or, in the modern day, from drug-altered states of consciousness. For the aesthetic, the ultimate test of living is winning through force and evil is weakness.

Ethical living is to be able to define the Good, and evil is ignorance of the Good. "The ethical hero is not the man of power, the man who does, but the philosopher, the man who knows." (Auden, 1952, p. 12) The victory of the ethical life is to do good rather than to feel good. The highest form of ethical expression is Stoic courage that transcends human vanity and fateful doom.

Choices 4 and 5 are Kierkegaard's religious choices. Choice 4 is commitment to immanence: the god within — absorption into solipsistic absolutism. Choice 5 is commitment to relationship with a transcendent deity not knowable as an object of consciousness but only as a presence that demands obedience.

Kierkegaard taxed the society of his times with the surrender of their responsibility for personal choice to public opinion. The effort to insure the harmonious functioning of society trivializes choice and the public-at-large rarely validates or appreciates demonstrations of transcendent *self*hood. This is a pseudo-problem. The real problem for modern society is the belief that all paradoxical questions should be decided by the scientific method. In the field of psychology this is the major threat to authenticity. Scientific determinism tells the individual that it guarantees the correct answer but the individual, deprived of choice, is still in despair. So, if one does not refuse all choice, the individual makes an irrelevant choice just to maintain the power of choice. In aesthetic living the individual justifies life by a serious commitment to aesthetic accomplishment. With the development of physical skills and creative talents, aesthetics offers a wide field for personal fulfillment. Aesthetic activity fails to give fulfillment, however, because it is subject to nullification by fate and misfortune. Then the individual turns to the ethical sphere to relieve despair.

From the ethical sphere one can propose solutions for the unhappiness that resulted from the unpredictable workings of nature in the aesthetic sphere. The ethical leads to despair, however, when social duty becomes the highest possible expression of choice. And, besides, the ethical position does not really reconcile one to accepting the loss of aesthetic enjoyment. The nonattachment of transcendence liberates the individual from despair over the shortcomings of the aesthetic and ethical solutions to the problems of living and from the dilemma of having to establish one of these as the absolute arbiter of *self*hood. Universal transcendence accomplishes this by providing goals that are independent of one's physical limitations and social roles. The problem for nonattachment is to keep freedom of choice from becoming a self-defining abstraction because then choice is again meaningless and one is again in despair. For Kierkegaard this raises the problem of sin, i.e., the appeal to some absolute other than God for justification. But whatever the transcendent agent that one chooses to obey, universal transcendence breaks down with the realization that there is *no* Other that has an authority which one does not give it.

41

The way out of this predicament is twofold. First, to accept the absurdity of the quest for absolute justification and remain passionately committed to the aesthetic and ethical in spite of their irreconcilable paradoxes, or, second, to risk everything on a passionate commitment to the unpredictable outcome of a human relationship. Now, it is absurd to think that all one's physical capacities, creative intelligence, social position, and cultural tradition are not only of no avail in this ultimate moment of trial but are in fact the true cause of one's predicament. And it is humiliating to think that one's destiny as a human being can only be redeemed by surrendering demands for self-validation in return for devotion to a particular person or cause that requires unquestioning obedience. This, according to Kierkegaard, is how one discovers one's own *self*hood and in this faith one can reclaim the experience of the aesthetic, ethical, and universal, which led to this decision, and live without despair, envy, and resentment.

Now of course, the question for Kierkegaard at this point is what happens to the Knight of Faith (the one who has discovered transcendent *self*hood) with the death of the beloved partner on whom the relationship depends, or, even worse, what happens if the beloved Guru, to whom you have just sworn everlasting obedience, tells you that he is the head of an international drug syndicate and your job will be to push dope. Or to be more mundane, what happens to the child when the parent whom he/she implicitly trusts and adores turns out to be a paranoid fiend or a sexual pervert. The answer to this problem is, first, that for the individual, grief, not despair, is the appropriate response to irreparable loss, and, second, that if one is in despair because of judging the behavior of others, then one is still in the ethical sphere; and Kierkegaard never suggested that the Knight of Faith had any right to make life-and-death choices for any one other than himself.

42

Speaking in Buffalo in 1946, Nora Waln related an incident which demonstrates this. Nora Waln, a Quaker and a dedicat-

ed pacifist, became internationally famous in the 1920's for her relief work with German youth suffering the hardships of post-war Germany. Some of the youth that she worked with became influential in the Nazi Party in the 30's and Miss Waln became well acquainted with Heinrich Himmler. By the outbreak of war in 1939 Miss Waln had left Germany and was in England preparing to publish a second book on the outcome of her relief work. At this point she received a letter from Himmler saying he wanted to talk to her about her new book and would she come to Berlin. So Miss Waln took an underground boat to Holland and was driven to Berlin in a Gestapo car. Himmler greeted her cordially and told her that his intelligence had obtained the galley proof of her new book and he had read things in there that he couldn't allow to be published. And, if she did not agree to withdraw the book he had a list of hostages to whom she was devotedly attached that he would execute. Himmler went on to express his admiration for Miss Waln personally and his gratitude for her service to Germans and he stated that he shared her ideals for a society of justice and respect for the individual. But, he said, you can't achieve this society by letting people have free choice. You have to force them to do what's good for the group. Miss Waln responded by saying that her commitment was to truth and telling the truth about the Nazis was more important to her than offending Himmler or even preserving the lives of her friends. And if he chose to execute her friends that was his choice and not hers. The interview was concluded. Miss Waln went back to England. Her book was published. And her friends were executed.

Now Kierkegaard's views on the ransoming of hostages (1941 a.) are well known to his readers. And one may question the morality of Miss Waln's action in that she appears to be as fanatical as Himmler but Kierkegaard would judge that both of them justified their choices. They were both passionately devoted to their causes. They made responsible choices; they were not in despair; and they were not asking for psychothera-py. The point for psychotherapists is that clients can only be treated for despair — not for moral transgressions. And it is not relevant to challenge Kierkegaard by asking him to justify the choices of Adolf Eichmann or Charles Colson or the fol-

43

lower of Jim Jones. The question is always to the reader: What do you intend to do with your life?

In the maturational process of *self*-identity, Kierkegaard has proposed that aesthetic living begins in the womb and progresses through various stages as the individual realizes that he has to make choices and is in despair when the blows of fate and misfortune prevent these choices from leading to satisfaction. The first stage ends by age six when the child realizes that magic does not control the real world — grandparents die, fathers and mothers get divorces, and illness is painful. In the second stage of aesthetic living, language and imagination provide a new strategy for control of enjoyment but even this cannot salvage the vision of aesthetic security. By the end of latency the child has had to choose between autistic withdrawal and ethical socialization.

A therapy that especially addresses itself to aesthetic despair is the Rational Emotive Therapy of Albert Ellis (1979). Ellis is the champion of ethical living as the solution for emotional problems. Ellis's therapy liberates the client from the bind of aesthetic paralysis by demonstrating the absurdity of surrendering life purpose to the workings of uncontrollable fate. Ellis denies the necessity of transference and insight and appeals to rational logic as the foundation of life purpose. Ellis ignores the reality of logical paradoxes and therefore sees no need for the discovery of *self*-transcendence.

Ethical socialization is a cultural strategy to overcome the aesthetic misfortunes of living and to assuage the ultimate aesthetic defeat of death. Religious institutions are the vehicles of consolation for this extremity. Religious institutions go beyond the limits of human ethics to invoke global transcendence; but in this process they negate social responsibility. Kierkegaard rejected global transcendence as a human goal and instead proposed a leap of faith that did not promise security in solipsistic oblivion but paradoxically intensified both the risks and satisfactions of human be-ing.

44

Most systems of therapy set their sights for human capacity no higher than moral conformity. Freud called this a "normal degree of misery." The ego-object psychologies, as well as the behavior therapies, are still tilling the solid ground of morality. The humanistic revolution has found many spaces of its own but earth is not one of them. Jung and Rank were the early prophets of transcendent liberation and Kohut is a beneficiary of their legacy. Kohut has shown that personality development proceeds along the two lines predicted by Kierkegaard. Aesthetic living is the resolution of grandiose childhood omnipotence and ethical living is the realization of the idealized image. The conjunction of these two lines of development produces Kohut's integrated self. Kohut does not make any claims for transcendence but he does place the Tragic Man of nuclear ambitions and ideals above the Guilty Man of instinctual drives and superego controls. Narrowly interpreted, Kohutian therapy might not lead beyond convincing the client that he or she is indeed a very special person living in a nurturing, protective universe. On the other hand, Kohut's two lines of development require only the vision of faith to attain transcendent *self*hood.

VII

THE LIFE OF FAITH

IN THIS CHAPTER I will describe a model of personality based on the process of faith. It is similar to Jung's and Heidegger's mandala models of intersecting complementary forces except that it faces uncompleted toward its future existence. The model is diagrammed in Figure 1, page 47. The domain of ego psychology encompasses ego-logic, on the right, attached to its product of object-images, on the left. Ego-logic is the center of the psyche that perceives and communicates with environment and directs the conscious functions of the body. It is the Adult ego state of Transactional Analysis. It is the analyzer and interpreter of perception and the author of the ego-object representations which comprise its object-self. The object-self on the left contains both good and bad objects, which are split in the pathological self. The Jungian "shadow" is the soft outer shell of the object-self and it too contains both positive and negative images.

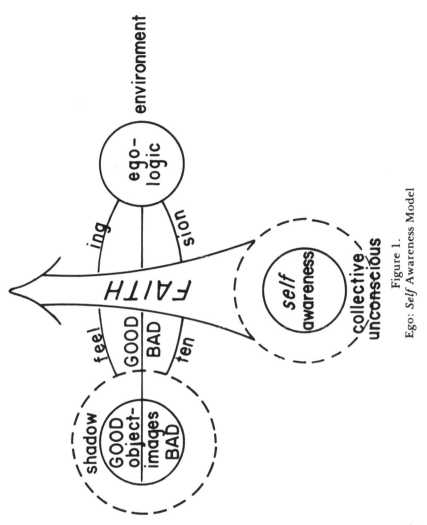

Figure 1.
Ego: *Self* Awareness Model

Feeling tension between ego-logic and ego-object arises from ego's opinions about its objects. Good feelings reflect ego's approval of good objects and bad feelings result from disapproval. Feelings of joy/sorrow, pain/pleasure, etc., are a product of ego-functioning and are transient feelings possessed by ego in the same way as ego owns its object-images. Moral therapy is principally concerned with alteration of feeling moods and behavioral adaptation to meet moral standards. Moral therapy is based on the idea that happiness results from social adaptation; and it reinforces the fallacy that psychic health is the repetition of good feelings and the extinction of bad feelings. The function of moral therapy is to educate and train ego to cooperate with its superego to achieve happiness. Moral therapy defines the unconscious as: What I can't know, and anything I don't have ego-permission to think about is consigned to the unconscious. Existentialism calls the refusal to recognize truths that I don't want to think about "bad faith."

Although existential therapy denies that moral behavior is the ultimate basis of human fulfillment, it by no means negates the obligation of ethical social behavior. It insists on *self*-expression that transcends moral behavior. Faithful *self*-expression emerges and is projected when ego can surrender its illusion that it is specially privileged to live in a nurturing and protective universe. The Biblical word for this change of mind is *metanoia* — usually translated as repentance. *Metanoia* has nothing to do with guilt over misconduct or negative feelings about bad ego-objects. Existential repentance is the change of mind which recognizes that all efforts to reform my private world of ego-objects is not going to have a damn bit of effect on the real universe that I ultimately have to deal with. So called "existential depression" is not based on the realistic appraisal of an unsympathetic universe. It is the despair of refusal to give up the expectation of validation of an illusory world. "Therapeutic" efforts to support the validity of indi-

48

vidual "specialness" in a nurturing universe not only do not deliver the promised happiness, but, as current gynecological research shows, the womb was never that perfect in the first place.

In Figure 1, *self* is shown adjacent to the domain of ego psychology. *Self,* however, has no location in static space. *Self* lives *in* time. It defines itself — not in terms of tangible objects that can be located in space — but by its own process of emergent expression. *Self* is a stranger to the domain of ego psychology with its assemblages of fixed measurable objects. *Self* cannot be made to surrender to scientific measurement because it makes its existence known not to anonymous machines but only spontaneously and unpredictably to another *self* in a moment of vision.

For accounts of the recognition of *self* one must turn to the literature of existential philosophy. *Self* is the experience of spontaneous consciousness identified by Sartre quoted in Chapter V. Van Dusen (1972) has described the hypnagogic experience of *self.* In meditational states, *self*-awareness appears as immediate, nonreflective consciousness. Nonreflective consciousness has been extensively discussed by Krishnamurti. In states of *self*-awareness, ego-reflective thinking is suspended and mind is alert to sensory stimuli. Krishnamurti puts it this way: "If there is a space between you and the thunder, you didn't hear the thunder" (1970, p. 86). That is *immediate* experience. In therapy free association is the verbalization of immediate feeling.

Self is surrounded by its neighbor, the collective unconscious. *Self* contributes to Jung's sensation : intuition polarity corresponding to ego participation in the thinking : feeling polarity. Jung's individuation denotes the mutual cooperation of ego and *self.*

49

Self manifests personal identity by faithful projection of Caring to human partners. The act of faith is the key that unlocks *self*-transcendence. Faith is not ego belief in illusory fantasy. It is projection of *self*-expression to make empathic contact; and faith refuses to withdraw even when rejected. It is the unique manifestation of a commitment to spiritual communion meeting and encompassing the be-ing of two individuals. To share my recognition that I have been loved and am able to accept that love is the transforming experience of therapy for both client and therapist.

A client expressed this to a therapist as follows: "I have been trying to think of how to express my gratitude to you for what has happened to me in therapy. All I can say is, that if we had never met, the *I* that is here now never would have existed."

CHAPTER VIII

I AND THOU

IN THE "I AND THOU,"
Buber envisioned the redemptive relationship of psychotherapy. The relationship of I and Thou is one in which two *selves* each project and mutually confirm each other's "secret evidence of a common destiny." Lain Entralgo calls this "believing love" (Seguin, 1965, p. 28). "Believing love" expresses a commitment to personal choice as the affirmation of *self*. And it confirms the existence of an ideal *self*-imago which comes to ego to give meaning to the struggle for aesthetic and ethical validation. The ideal *self*-imago is not provided from without, as would be seen by ego, for whom *self* is only another object which ego can observe but never be. The ideal *self*-imago is born by the being of the individual. It is the destiny of the individual to express this *self* to the Thou who will understand and confirm him. The therapist is such an individual. He projects a caring *self* in the faith that the client will understand and validate him. And he does not retreat when

the client misunderstands him. The client misunderstands him because his life-striving until now has been to get the world to invest him with a *self*. Yet all the object-selves the world has provided have only served to aggravate his emptiness, longing, and isolation—shameful defects he brings to the therapist to repair.

In the analytic transference the client attacks the therapist for failing to provide the affection that his or her parents withheld. In countertransference the therapist attacks the client for failing to meet his affective needs. Transference is projection of the guilt felt for attacking oneself. The analytic therapist interprets this to the client and persuades him to forgive himself. Kohut's mirror transference (1971) does not focus on guilt. Mirror transference is the creation of a relationship of transcendent *self*-communion between therapist and client.

Laing (1969, a,b) describes the predicament of the schizoid who exhausts himself collecting the object-images he uses to represent (not project) himself. For this client, who comes to therapy to plunder the therapist of his power and love, therapy is an agonizing test of endurance which can only end, when the client, finally bursting in to "rob the bank," finds the vault door wide open and the "money" there for the taking. But the client *I*, who here truly meets the partner's *Thou*, now understands that he has no need for the "money." He understands that the *self* which he *is*—that *self*—is revealed in his action, in contrast to the psuedo-self which is merely represented by ego-images.

In the creative process of contacting the other, according to Perls, Hefferline, and Goodman (1951), the fragmented figure-ground coalesces and an integrated bright figure emerges to satisfy organismic excitement. They state "In the [goal of] final contact the self is immediately and fully engaged in the *figure* it has discovered-and-invented; momentarily there is practically no background. The figure embodies all the concern of the self and the self is nothing [sic] but its present concern, so the self *is* the figure." (1951, p. 416)

The enterprise of Gestalt Therapy is to confront individuals with the ways in which they interrupt the creative process short of final contact (*self*hood). When therapy is successful, the individual experiences the interrupting process as his own creation. Awareness (of the interruption) one has been avoiding emerges and now becomes the bright figure that closes the gestalt; and the individual experiences the creative process as *happening of its own accord.*

The existential therapist believes with Sartre that

Human reality is its own transcending toward what it lacks; it transcends itself toward the particular being which it would be if it were what it is. . . . It exists first as lack . . . and emerges as a presence in the world . . . apprehended by itself as *its* own lack . . . transcending toward a coincidence with itself which is never [a] given.

The act by which a feeling becomes conscious of its exact nature, limits and defines itself — this act is one and the same as the act by which it presents itself with a transcendent object. The affective state, *being consciousness,* cannot exist without a transcendent correlative. When feeling is oriented toward something real, actually perceived, the thing, like a reflector, returns the light it has received. . . . As a result of this continual interaction, the feeling is continually enriched at the same time as the object soaks up affective qualities. . . . Each affective quality is so deeply incorporated in the object that it is impossible to distinguish between what is felt and what is perceived.

In the constitution of the *unreal* object, knowledge plays the role of perception. . . . Thus the unreal object emerges. . . . Only this unreal, so well specified and defined, is empty; or rather it is the simple reflection of the feeling. (1965, pp. 170, 89).

Heidegger writes:

53

Da-sein means *being projected* into Nothing. Projecting into Nothing, *Da-sein* is already beyond what-is-in-totality. This "being beyond" what-is we call Transcendence. Were *Da-sein* not, in its essential basis, transcendent, that is to say, were it not projected from the start into Nothing, it could never relate to what-is, hence could have no self-relationship. Without the original manifest character of Nothing there is no self-hood and no freedom. (1949, p. 399)

Seguin presents the theme that the curative movement of therapy is the sharing of "positive-loving-feelings *between two human beings*" (1965, p. 124). He goes on to write:

[This] experience is full of beauty and rejoicing . . . [arising] from the vibration of two persons in unison, who, thanks to and joined in love, have discovered a new horizon. . . . It is a communion fundamentally different from communication and of foremost importance in all real human intimacy.

This difficult and impossible communion in which two selves incur the dread of projecting themselves into the unknown outcome of intimate meeting is the burden and the reward of psychotherapy. From this meeting two new selves are born, enriched, and liberated.

Martin Buber (1958, p. 109) has described transcendent meeting as follows:

What is the eternal, primal phenomenon, present here and now . . . which we term revelation? It is that [meeting from which] man does not pass . . . the same being as he entered into it. . . . [It is] not an "experience" that stirs in the receptive soul and grows to perfect blessedness; rather, in that moment something *happens* to the man. . . . The man who emerges from the act of pure relation that so involves his being has now in his being something more that has grown in him, of which he did not know before and whose origin he is not rightly able to indicate. However the source of this new thing is classified in the scientific orientation of the world, with its authorized efforts to establish an unbroken causality, we, whose concern is real consideration of the real, cannot have our purpose served with subconsciousness or any other apparatus of the soul. The reality is that we receive what we did not heretofore have, and receive it in such a way that we *know* it has been given to us. (Author's italics)

For ego, time is the domain of infinite, regular, demonstrable movement. For *self*, time is the experience of spontaneous, unpredictable, inexhaustible living. To be authentically human the individual must know both poles of this dialectic. Authentic human be-ing reveals the connection between these poles by leaping ahead, in imagination, to death — that moment when my life stops and "time" goes on. This future moment is seen by *self* and only awaited by ego. Biological death occurs uniquely but psychic stoppage of the sense of flow-of-time — the experience of anxiety — is a common experience of life. Linear deterministic therapy looks to discover the causes of anxiety; existential therapy teaches how to arrest its process.

Ego is the central agent in a psychic world of irreducible, self-defining drives and time-independent facts. *Self*, from which human be-ing derives authentic meaning and personal identity, arises in its response to the world of historical experience. Ego loses *self* in its effort to invest an absurd world with meaning. The reward for the success of this effort is neurosis; the penalty for failure is depression. Depression is the response of ego when time is overwhelming. Thus, the enterprise of therapy is to facilitate the process of *self*-discovery, which choicefully propels the individual through the present moment while uniting the past with the future.

IX

AWARENESS AND
RESPONSIBILITY

THE GENESIS OF GES-
talt Therapy is largely credited to the genius of Frederick
Perls. His method of therapy is to bring into *self*-awareness
the ways in which the person interrupts contact with other
human beings. For Perls, awareness dictated responsibility.
Perls worked in New York, Florida, and California without
attracting much professional notice until he began to train
groups of therapists at the Esalen Institute in the 1960s. Aided
by the burgeoning interest in growth groups and the impact
of his charismatic leadership, Perls became widely known and
left an indelible impression on hundreds of therapists who
worked with him.

56   Perls began to criticize psychoanalytic treatment principles in a book published in 1945 entitled *Ego, Hunger and
Aggression*. Perls's observation was that psychoanalysis devoted major attention to cognitive character structures and failed
to appreciate the gains that could be achieved by transform-

ing anxiety into excitement. A later book, *Gestalt Therapy, Excitement and Growth in Human Personality* (1951), further develops this idea. Perls's associates have added much about the practice of Gestalt Therapy, but a method that is essentially based on techniques for letting go of ego defenses to allow the emergence of *self*-awareness does not require extensive theories of intrapsychic mechanisms. On the contrary, Perls customarily devastated those who failed to stay with the experiential contact boundary because the therapist was missing opportunities for empathic contact and at the same time was teaching the client to avoid contact.

Avoidance of contact by the client was for Perls (1973) the key to the exposure of pathology. He described four types of contact avoidance — projection, introjection, retroflection, and confluence. The introjector swallows input whole without chewing and ends up with a stomach ache. Projectors blame others for behavior they are responsible for. Confluence is lack of boundary awareness. Confluent persons behave "as if" they are in contact with the environment. Retroflectors are unwilling to express their needs to others and compound their suffering by punishing themselves for cowardice. Then they say "Poor me." Self-awareness makes contact with the environment and allows the individual the possibility of expressing cut-off capacities.

Lupe is a client from the author's practice who forcefully makes her presence known in group by maintaining an imperious silence. Her face displays the pain of narcissistic self torture. Lupe is an experienced "bear trapper." Efforts by the therapist to make contact with her during these periods are frequently met by rebuff. After one of these rebuffs the therapist switched his attention to another member of the group and Lupe became openly incensed. "I can't believe you don't know what you just did," she stormed. The therapist replied that he had done several things during the previous few minutes and that he didn't know which thing she was objecting to. Her reply, expressing intense anger was, "Bullshit." The therapist replied that he was

57

only willing to invest a certain amount of energy in attempting to penetrate her wall and that he had intentionally stopped trying to get some response from her but that he was now very interested in working with her expressed anger. Whereupon, she became passive again and said that she had given up trying to convince people of the reality of her feelings. In fact, they felt unreal to her too and she only felt real behind the protection of her wall. The therapist asked her if anybody she knew was phoney. She failed to name anyone and the therapist asked her if she was willing to experiment by loudly saying, "You're a phoney therapist." She did this several times in successively louder tones and then broke into a laugh. When asked what amused her she said, "My mother always told me never to raise my voice."

This is an illustration of dissolving confluence by a Gestalt Therapy technique. The client is in contact with the wall that separated her from the feeling of anger but says there is "nothing" on the other side of the wall. This is Perls's (1969) implosive dead layer. Lupe was not willing to examine or own her feeling of anger and frustration over her "phoney" expression but the therapist got her to project it onto him. As she did this, her mother's injunction "Don't raise your voice" emerged and her wall of body tension dissolved.

Ruth is a social work student intern supervised by the author. She was playing a tape of the third session with a family in therapy. She opened with this statement: "I was thinking about our last session. I was relieved to see you fighting a little bit there. You had all been so polite to each other before. It didn't feel quite real. I've been thinking about that." Her last sentence, "I've been thinking about that," trailed off into an embarrassed laugh and she said to her supervisor, "That was a terrible speech. It sounded so canned." The supervisor asked her what she was feeling and she said she was feeling embarrassed at her stupid remark. The supervisor asked her to imagine that she was back with her clients and saying instead "I don't feel real in here." As she said this to the supervisor she broke out laughing and said, "Yes, that's it. I don't feel real as I ask them to be real with me."

58

Following this she was able to listen to the tape and see the reality of the resistive pattern of this family. The appropriation of her felt sense produced a body-shift and changed the direction of her attention from her sense of "unreality" to the family interaction in the session. In both of these examples the therapist has guided the client to bypass resistance and experience the release of body tension.

Gestalt Therapy works with the process of experiencing — the translation of feeling into thought that the client can recognize. Analytic therapy translates the client's behavior into concepts that the therapist asks the client to adopt. The client may experience a body-shift by adopting the concept the therapist has presented but the client depended on the therapist to do the work. In Gestalt Therapy, therapist ego does not lead client ego and does not do for client ego what clients' egos can do for themselves.

The individual's defensive avoidance reveals itself in his misuse of pronouns. When the introjector says, "I think," he usually means "they think" (Perls 1973, p. 35). When the projector says "it" or "they" he usually means "I" (p. 37). The anonymous "we" is used by the confluent client who is including himself indiscriminately with the whole world. The retroflector uses the pronoun "myself" as though he were two different people as in "I am ashamed of myself" (p. 41).

Perls (1969) also pointed out that the client's body language provided valuable clues to the impasse that was blocking *self*-expression. He described the therapeutic process as one of penetrating through the personality layers that suppress excitement. The first layer is the token contact between the organism and the environment from which it seeks support. This is the layer of pastiming and superficial relationship. The second layer is the attempt to achieve support through games, roles, and maneuvers which lead to unresolved conflict and emotional distress. Beneath this layer is the phobic impasse of immobilization and unrelieved anxie-

59

ty. Faced with the loss of environmental support, and failing to produce self-support, the individual shuts off the sense of flow of time by holding-in. Breath holding is a manifestation of holding-in—a resistance to spontaneity. Principally one holds-in anger, grief, joy, and orgasm. This is the implosive or death layer. Self-support is realized when the individual expresses feelings of excitement and understands their meaning.

The Gestalt therapist focuses on the sensory capacities which the client disowns in order to avoid the responsibility for refusing environmental contact. When the client takes responsibility for his methods of refusing environmental support, the impasse becomes the missing figure of attention and he is free to express *self*hood.

X

DECIDING TO CHANGE

WHEN AN INDIVIDUAL
becomes aware of his responsibility for deciding on a life purpose, he is able to enter into authentic relationships and live
without despair, envy, and resentment. Mary and Robert
Goulding (1979) have described the process of deciding to
change in their book *Changing Lives Through Redecision
Therapy*. The Gouldings name authentic choices *contracts*.
The therapeutic contract is an agreement between two individuals for each to take responsibility for his part in reaching
an agreed-on behavioral goal. The client's contract is an
agreement with himself or herself. The therapist's contract is
to be responsible—to be *there*—to the client. Being *there* is
the essence of faithful contact. The therapist is responsible for
his own be-ing, not the be-ing of the client. The work of therapy is to overcome the obstacles which interrupt contact between client and therapist as the client works toward his goal.

61

The end of therapy is that the client be able to ask for and to negotiate with others for what he or she wants.

Therapy governed by an authentic contract does not degenerate into pastiming about feeling moods and ego-objects. The contract likewise does not honor neurotic Games that attempt to translate the past into the future while avoiding the present. The terms of the contract are How and Now. The basis of any authentic contract is to live Now. The first order of therapeutic work, therefore, is to discover whether the client has a secret archaic contract to kill himself when he finds he cannot be specially privileged to claim magical protection. Faithful therapy demands that the therapist not only must not give the client permission to claim magical protection but must not claim it for himself.

The Gouldings' term for archaic protection/destruction contracts is Injunctions. Injunctions are parental messages accepted by the client in childhood that decree the conditions for avoiding caring contact with another human being. Injunctions are always prescriptions for *not* living: Don't be, Don't be close, Don't grow, Don't be male/female, Don't succeed, etc. Injunctions are the successors to the witch's curse and the individual who accepts the Injunction goes through life with a neurotic handicap.

Along with the injunctive curse, the parent also supplies a counterinjunctive charm that suspends the Injunction. The charm, however, is paradoxically just as bad as the curse. A typical counter-Injunction might be: You won't die if you publish a book or change jobs every year. A counter-Injunction for "Don't love" would be: "You won't be unhappy if you go to bed with every man/woman you meet."

The principle of not–be-ing is called the Racket. A person's Racket is the way in which he or she goes through life postponing authentic choice (Edwards, 1972). The currency of the Racket is the Stamp. A Stamp is the token of postponed feeling choice. Bad feeling Stamps are postponed bad feelings

62

and Good feeling Stamps are postponed good feelings. Examples of these are: I can't afford to get mad at my boss so I postpone feeling angry until I can discharge it at my wife/child/dog. Or: I can't afford to enjoy myself until I save my money, finish my work, etc. When I come to cash in the Stamp, the promised satisfaction turns out to be counterfeit.

The client's life is at an impasse until he breaks his secret contract to withhold *self*-expression. The purpose of Redecision Therapy is to discover the secret contract and let the client decide how he wants to change it. The Gouldings analyze impasses according to the personality structure of Transactional Analysis: "The first-degree impasse is between the Parent ego state of the individual and his Child ego state and is based on the counter-Injunctions" (1979, p. 45). The first-degree impasse is broken by deciding to no longer invoke the magic charm which was supposed to suspend the Injunction but which is really killing him anyway. The man who believes he won't die if he publishes a book every year comes to therapy with high blood pressure, physical exhaustion, depression, and a failing marriage. Before he decides to give up the counter-Injunction he needs to make a clear contract not to honor the Injunction to kill himself. Otherwise he runs the risk of leaving the treatment session in a euphoric glow of liberation only to drive into a fatal accident on the freeway.

A second-degree impasse springs from a childhood decision by the client to counteract the lethal parental Injunction. That is, the client makes the decision to believe in neither curses nor charms and proceeds to live without the benefit of fantasy, spontaneity, and playfulness, which are necessary for authentic be-ing. This client presents himself as one who has been a grown-up adult all his life. When the client is able to own the unexpressed grief and anger for his or her unfulfilled childhood, the impasse will be overcome.   *63*

According to the Gouldings (1979, p. 47), "The third-degree impasse is one in which the patient experiences himself as *always* having been whatever it is he experiences. . . . He was 'born' that way, he states." In the third-degree impasse the client denies the existence of the positive side of every polarity. He can only be the negative or bad side. This impasse can be broken by having the client play both sides of his polarity until he is able to be responsible for connecting the two.

In the theory of Transactional Analysis, "stroking" is the essence of caring contact as well as the basis for human survival. Stroking is social response that either validates or discounts *self*hood. One of the purposes of therapy is to teach the client to give, to accept, and to ask for positive strokes. Stroke hunger is the need for recognition, excitement, and physical contact. Positive strokes reinforce *self*-expression and promote social cooperation. Negative strokes discourage *self*-consciousness and interfere with social cooperation. A negative stroke is a *self*-discount — a "don't be" Injunction. Goulding (1980) states that when persons don't know how to get positive strokes they continue their self-defeating behavior to punish both others and themselves for not getting them. They do not, however, see negative strokes as an acceptable substitute for positive strokes.

Schiff (1971) has described four ways of discounting:

1) Discount the problem. Example: The baby is crying. The mother turns up the radio or goes to sleep.

2) Discount the significance of the problem. Example: The baby is crying. The mother says, "He always cries this time of the day."

3) Discount the solvability of the problem. Example: The baby is crying. Mother says, "Nothing satisfies him."

4) Discount the person. Example: The baby is crying. The mother says, "There's nothing I can do."

64   Negative strokes are the carriers of "Don't exist" injunctions, such as Don't think, Don't feel, Don't touch, Don't need, or Don't be lovable. The negative injunctions adopted by the child form the basis of neurotic pathology. Positive

strokes tell individuals that they are valuable, useful, intelligent, lovable, and that the world is friendly.

Throughout the lifetime of the individual, physical strokes are crucial to a sense of well-being. In infancy physical strokes are the prime medium of communication between parent and child. A severe deficit of positive strokes for the infant is known to produce the failure-to-thrive syndrome. Infant stimulation has been shown to be critical for normal brain development in the first 18 months of life as well as for maternal-child bonding and development of trusting relationship. Children get strokes from playing—by themselves and with others. The child who does not learn to play fails to experience aesthetic fulfillment. His possibilities in the aesthetic sphere are not realized and he gets to the ethical sphere with a maturational deficit. As an adult he fails to read nonverbal communications from others and he has difficulty in expressing affective warmth by nonverbal means. In old age (second childhood) physical strokes again become crucial to life-support and relatively more important than intellectual strokes.

The next stage of stroke stimulation for the child is stroking for intellectual and thinking performance. Responsibility means that one can make contracts and keep promises and predict the consequences of one's behavior as well as that of parental authority and peer companions. This is essential for satisfactory maturation in the ethical sphere. The individual who accepts a "Don't think" Injunction is in despair because he is ethically crippled. The acme of stroke reward is intimacy —a spiritual sharing that transcends aesthetic and ethical satisfaction. For the individual who is in despair over failure to attain aesthetic and ethical maturity, intimacy can only be a distant, tantalizing phantom—described in art, praised by enthusiasts, and an empty promise to the sufferer. For these reasons, Re-parenting (Schiff, 1972), is an important treatment modality in T.A. therapy. Through Re-parenting, the

65

grown-up client is given a second chance to experience the maturational choices that were missed the first time around.

The stroke "mix," and the Injunctions that justify the stroke "mix," form the basis for the Life Script that the child decides to adopt. Life Scripts are story plots that tell the child what he must do to survive in the world (Berne, 1972). Unsatisfying and unrewarding behaviors that the child practices are performed to justify a pathological Life Script, and, of course, to maintain amicable relations with the significant others who view him as a non-*self*. The Script belongs to the aesthetic stage of the child's life experience and is legacy of the Child ego state. The Script is the Child's plan for attaining *self*hood: The Script, like the fairy tale, embodies the wisdom of the intuitive preconscious. Fairy tales do not analyze or explain behavior. Witches are evil because they are witches. Consequences are not causally linked to behavior. People suffer because they are cursed and enjoy good fortune because they are charmed. People act their parts because they are assigned to them by fate. But after one struggles through the trials set for one by fate one achieves transcendent *self*hood.

The life positions prescribed by the Script define one's relationship to others. There are four life positions:

1) I'm O.K.: You're O.K.
2) I'm *not* O.K.: You're O.K.
3) I'm O.K.: You're *not* O.K.
4) I'm *not* O.K.: You're *not* O.K.

In number 1, two Adult ego states see each other as O.K. In numbers 2, 3, and 4, the voices that speak are those of Child and Parent ego states, each berating the other and/or condemning themselves. An ego state is a coherent, identifiable, durable constellation of behavioral characteristics. An ego state is manifestly identified by language, voice, feeling states, gestures, and transactional roles. The Child ego state is the outcome of the aesthetic maturational process to age 6. The Parent ego state is the outcome of the ethical maturational process to age 12. Adult is the outcome of the adolescent maturational process and is *self*-emergence in the process of intimate commitment to an Other.

The Child and Parent are archaic states while the Adult is chronologically present-oriented. In T.A. therapy one is liberated from his pathological (self-destructive) Script when one's transcendent Adult *self* emerges. In this process, one reclaims the unfinished maturational tasks from the aesthetic and ethical and redecides one's Life Script based on the capacity for transcendent Adult relationships. T.A.'s teaching method of diagramming transactions is a visual means of promoting change from the aesthetic (Child) sphere and the ethical (Parent) sphere to the transcendent (Adult) sphere. This is attested to by the therapeutic success of T.A. practitioners as well as by the immense popularity of Berne's book *Games People Play* (1964).

Games, Stamps, and Rackets are pathological symptomatology through which the individual justifies inauthenticity (non*self*hood). The Game is a repetitive reenactment of a Parent-Child conflict that provides each player with a familiar disagreeable payoff. The payoff is the name of the Game. Child payoffs are typically abused, helpless, not-O.K. positions such as Kick-Me, Stupid, and See What You Made Me Do. Parent payoffs are frustrated, punitive positions such as Now I've Got You and When Will You Ever Learn? The interlocking Parent-Child Game payoffs portray a paradoxical ego conflict which neither party can resolve because the Parent and Child positions are archaic positions fixed in time by unresolved conflicts. Therapy consists in persuading a player to get out of the Game by shifting to Adult present-time, in-the-room contact.

The Game transaction consists of five steps:

1) An ostensible Adult 1 to Adult 2 transaction.
2) A secret Child 1 to Parent 2 cross-transaction.
3) A negative Parent 2 to Child 1 response.

4) The Payoff feeling for the Child 1 and the Parent 2 ego states.

5) Surprised Adult 1,2 reactions to the outcome. (Goulding, 1978)

An example of a Game is:

> *The husband is late dressing to go out to dinner. He says to his wife, "Have you seen my cufflinks?" If this were a legitimate Adult-to-Adult Transaction she might say, "Check the shirt you wore last night," or simply, "No, I haven't," and that would be the end of the transaction. The Game commences when the wife's Parent hears an implied message from the husband's Child: "You ought to take better care of me." The wife then responds from her Parent. "Look for your own cufflinks, I'm tired of taking care of you." The husband's payoff is Kick Me; and the wife's payoff is Why am I surrounded by helpless people?*

At this point husband's and wife's Adults express surprise at the outcome of the transaction. When games are played between clients in a group session, it is helpful for the participants to look at the satisfactions they realize from being helpless or from being extra helpful. The function of the Game is to justify the *not*-O.K. position stipulated by the player's Script.

The existential foundation of Transactional Analysis is Berne's (1961) definition of personal relationship in terms of time structure. He stated that each individual divides his lifetime between six choices: 1) withdrawal 2) pastimes 3) ritual 4) activities 5) Games and 6) Intimacy. Withdrawal is a narcissistic or autistic state of relationship which can range from a serious commitment to self-examination to hiding in autistic avoidance of contact. Pastimes are superficial social encounters that deny authentic *self*hood but allow one to avoid despair. Rituals are social encounters that promote a sense of confluence without interpersonal commitment, i.e., public celebrations in which all the members of the audience are nominally committed to the group but express this only by ritualistic ceremony. Activities are goal-oriented tasks that meet demonstrable aesthetic or ethical objectives, i.e., painting a picture, playing professional football, inventing an artificial heart, or getting elected to public office. Activities, successfully pursued, can generate a *self*hood that is completely satisfying for the individual. Games represent the conflict which arises between Child and Parent ego states in the effort to force the Other to take away his/her despair. Games never liberate one from despair. Child and Adult in despair continue to accuse the other of being Not O.K., i.e., unsatisfying. Liberation, in T.A. terms, comes when Adult transcendence takes charge of existence and Child and Parent are able to see each other as being O.K., in spite of their defects. Intimacy is realized when one O.K. individual enters into a *self*-defining relationship with another O.K. individual. Only then does transcendent *self*hood emerge.

CHAPTER XI

HOW REAL IS CHOICE

IN WHAT HAS BECOME a series of books, Paul Watzlawick and his co-authors (1967, 1974, 1976, 1978) have been expanding the position that basing one's choice of behavior on the accepted certainties of culturally defined reality is a risky business. An even more serious mistake is to act as though an unintelligible communication is intelligible. Redundant choice systems in which the outcome is predetermined, and no real choice for change is possible, are a major source of pathology. Indeterminate choice systems, which provide several outcomes but allow no way of estimating their relative value, are another type of pathological communication. In the behavioral interrelation of self, message, and reality, the existential *self* of intuitive experience can play a crucial role in counteracting pathologic communication. A common characteristic of pathological communications is that they are closed or redundant. A redundant system is self-equilibrating and self-correcting, no matter what disturbance is imposed upon it. Redundant circuits are the foundation of control and guidance systems. They screen out and extinguish competing signals, noise, and random fluctuations. In human communication the effect of redundancy is to insure that no real choice for change is possible. While redundant guidance systems are essential for sending space ships to Mars, their adoption by human being produces pathologic behavior. The self that uses open communication channels is the *self* of autonomous existential choice. It arises out of its own concern, which it consciously confirms, in every situation in which it finds itself. In this moment of *self*-discovery, *self* seeks no other support. It is a self-defining intelligence.

Intelligence can be understood as either a self-defining agent or a self-defining message. The context of a communication, which defines how the language of the message is to be understood, is derived from a higher-order viewpoint than that in which the words themselves are stated. This viewpoint is derived from the context of experience which we call reality. In order to communicate, therefore, it is necessary to know what the communicating parties' assumptions are about reality.

Therapeutic problem-solving starts with identifying problems to be avoided. These come under the headings of problems of redundant systems. First among these are unmet demands that the universe justify itself. The idea that "somebody up there must be in charge" and that He can be called to account for His unfair or irrational behavior leads to the conclusion that a betrayal has taken place. The client will then think that either God, nature, or the universe has betrayed him, for which he wants revenge, or that he has betrayed them and well merits his suffering. For therapists presented with this kind of problem by clients, the Book of Job in the Old Testament can be very instructive. The lesson it teaches

71

is that the universe eventually answers for itself and that the scientific helpers who essay to speak for the universe just muddy up the waters. What the therapist can properly do is to engage the client's interest in making current decisions rather than waiting for ultimate answers.

Less absolute than God but no less frustrating are monolithic social institutions. In disputes with these institutions a good lawyer can provide better advice than a psychotherapist and may indeed win a resolution to a problem involving welfare benefits, disability compensation, or rights to fair and equal treatment in public facilities.

Taking on contests with valueless or rigged goals is a sure road to impasse. Most clients pose the problem more subtly than the query of the type "How can you do brain surgery, if you've never operated on yourself?", but the proposition that only a failure can treat a failure is not something to argue with the client about. The more subtle way the therapist gets hooked is in explaining "why the client has failed" and making helpful suggestions that the client does not execute. The yes-but and why-because systems are first-order redundant systems that lead nowhere. Eric Berne (1976) meant client choice, not "case progress" when he said, "Effective therapy is like a poker game. There is never any doubt about whether you've won or lost." I am not suggesting that clients' impossible demands be rejected; on the contrary, clients are disclosing to the therapist the existential world of frustration and futility they want to break out of.

Watzlawick posits several dialectical ways of classifying communication. One of these is first-order vs. second- and higher-order communication types; another is digital vs. analog communication modes. First-order communication limits itself to manipulating patterns of summative information. A property of summative combinations is that no matter what different patterns are established the final state is completely determined by the initial conditions (1967, p. 129). It

72

is a requirement of scientific experiment, for instance, that all properties of a system be fully and independently defined and all agents entering and leaving the system be fully accounted for. Science occasionally produces surprises but it leaves nothing to chance. In second-and higher-order communication new gestalts are discovered and invented that could not have been predicted from the summative properties of the systems.

"Digital communication" (1967, p. 60) is a term taken from computer technology that refers to off-on signals or information "bits." Digital signals offer a maximum degree of abstract discrimination. Analog signals, on the other hand, communicate information about the magnitude of effects occuring in a given situation. A telephone number, for instance, is a purely digital way of locating receiving terminal. The DSM *Manual of Mental Disorders* is a digital system for distinguishing among different summatively defined diseases. In human communication, "[a]nalog messages are invocations of relationship and are therefore proposals regarding the future rules of relationship" (1967, p. 101), whereas digital messages are denotative, declarative, or assertive. The power of *self*-disclosure is the ability to fluently express nonverbal analog messages in meaningful digital terms. "Psychotherapy is undoubtedly concerned with the correct and corrective digitalization of the analogic" (1967, p. 100). Experiential methods of therapy such as Gestalt Therapy are particularly concerned with dramatizing and verbalizing (digitalizing) nonverbal expressions of the analogic. Healthy behavior is an integrated expression of analogic and digital information. The sentence "I love my mother" is digital information that cannot be completely meaningful without taking into account the analogic component that confirms how much love is being expressed for mother. A negative shaking of the head or a disgusted smile that denies the digital assertion of love is pathological communication. The analog message is an ex-

73

pression of the meaning of the immediate situation in which the individual finds himself. Like art, psychotherapy conveys an analog communication. It is received and understood uniquely by each individual and it invites the receiver to know that he has been understood by another human being. Mismatched digital and analog messages cause a great deal of misunderstanding. Digital messages are "road maps." They identify and locate objects being talked about. The associated analog message tells why the places on the map are important to the individual and why the individual wants to travel from one place to another. A communication which produces misunderstanding results when speaker A puts out a digital "road map" and invites speaker B to guess where speaker A wishes to go. Speaker B plays the Game by supplying a destination and speaker A responds by saying, "Why would I want to go to City X when you know I like City Y better?" Speaker B then responds by saying, "But the road to City X is shorter, faster, more scenic, etc." and uproar commences. *Who's Afraid of Virginia Woolf?* illustrates this kind of misunderstanding.

In therapy, particularly group therapy, this game is sometimes known as Hunting for the Easter Eggs. Here the client or therapist puts out a digital message and the game players try to guess what the congruent analog message is while the game "director" sits back and says, "No, that's not it," to the interpretations provided. The game can also be played in reverse by furnishing unsolicited analog interpretations of expressed digital messages.

One way to interrupt this mismatch is to produce another "road map" which requires the hearer to produce a new analog message. Watzlawick calls this "Reframing" (1974, p. 92–109). An example quoted by Watzlawick is that of a police officer in Oakland, California, who found himself surrounded by an angry ghetto mob as he was handing a citation to a driver who had committed a traffic infraction. The officer

74

turned to the crowd and said in a loud voice, "You have just witnessed the issuance of a traffic ticket by a member of your Oakland Police Department." And, while the crowd was attempting to fathom the deeper meaning of this pronouncement, the officer got in his cruiser and drove off.

Many examples of the use of Reframing in therapy are given in the last part of *Change* (Watzlawick, 1974). A therapeutic procedure for dealing with confusing, incongruent digital-analog messages is, for example:

1) Identify and separate the digital and analog messages.

2) Refrain from interpreting or guessing the missing message.

3) Focus attention on the speaker's immediate, possibly nonverbal, analog message which relates to the in-the-room encounter.

4) Propose an "Experiment" with the purpose of getting the speaker to produce a digital "road map" that matches the present analog message.

Gestalt experiments (Naranjo, 1973) in which the client takes the parts of both polarities are particularly helpful for reaching congruent digital and analog messages. When this procedure produces a digital match with the speaker's inadequately expressed analog message, the speaker's confusion-conflict disappears; attention is freed for in-the-room contact and one no longer projects the confusion on the hearer. This realization of contact is understood as awareness. In the experience of the author, the attempt to produce an analog message that matches a confusing out-of-the-room digital message is much less likely to succeed.

"Conscious use of self" by the therapist functions as follows:

1) The therapist attends to his own experience of confusion with the incongruent messages.

2) The therapist avoids the response which denies or projects the confusion. That is, the therapist does not respond by

making a statement or asking a question that implies that the speaker's message makes sense.

3) The therapist also avoids an interpretation which assumes the responsibility for telling the speaker "what he really means."

Thus "conscious use of self" means conscious acceptance of one's own confusion, willingness to tolerate one's confusion, and not taking the responsibility for resolving the confusion away from the speaker, who then assumes the responsibility for producing a congruent message.

The substance of change is polarity. There is no uniquely detached fulcrum of truth with the objective observer perched on its infinitely fine apex. There are, however, *meta*-positions relative to systems from which the polarities encompassed by the systems can be defined, even as the new *meta*-polarity vis-à-vis the first system can be seen from a higher *meta*-position. The existential therapist does not, however, ascend a *meta*-escalator to cloudland. The purpose is to see what is existentially *there*. The first task is to clarify the polarities that are operating in the system that the client presents; second, to define the change to be achieved; and, third, to formulate a plan to produce this change.

The options are:

1) *Exaggerate the polarity to absurdity.* Carl Whitaker (1975) is particularly good at exposing and dramatizing polarities. An example Frankl (1963) gives is of the man who was bothered by sweating. Frankl asked him how much he estimated that he might sweat in a day. When the client gave Frankl a figure, Frankl prescribed the task of doubling the amount.

2) *Redraw the system boundary to include a workable polarity and exclude an unworkable polarity.* A therapist recalls an instance when he feared that an unstable paranoid patient might become violent. He left the room and called in his col-

league who immediately said to the patient, "I know just how you feel. I've often wanted to kill John myself."

3) *Rename the polarities of the present system.* Virginia Satir (1964) is especially skillful at doing this. She will reframe a client's expression of hostility into an expression of concern that the client will accept.

4) *Contract the system to bring a polarity into focus.* A therapist recounts the example of a client who was describing some diffuse paranoid fears. He said to him, "You know, I'm concerned that you're not suspicious enough. I think you should be paying closer attention to what your family is saying about you at home."

5) *Restore a denied polarity.* Jim Simkin (1974) would ask a patient who complained of being too shy to brag about his modesty.

Paradoxical problem-resolution utilizes the client's need for vindication and supports the motivation to rebel and resist; and it redirects it. The underlying theme of paradoxical intervention is to formulate choices which produce a higher-order change than is permitted by the client's unrewarding redundant system. In a paradoxical intervention the therapist goes with the client's resistance. For example, the therapist would agree with the client that the client's problem is irremediable and offer the client unbounded support with which to sustain the distress which he has incurred through no fault of his own. This may propel the client through the ethical or aesthetic impasse to a *meta*-position of nonattachment. If the client is really perverse the client will "one-up" the therapist by getting well in spite of the therapist's helplessness. The second-order change is that the therapist is presented as even more helpless than the client to discover the meaning of the symptom. In doing this the therapist redirects the client's efforts from an attempt to control the symptom to an attempt to control the therapist. Faced with the choice be-

77

tween attempting to control the therapist or themselves, clients find it more satisfying to control themselves. Real choice is made between an obvious polarity that arises from intuitive experience. The illusion of choice, which demands that one make a selection from a series of preformulated alternatives, denies the validity of intuitive experience and has no curative potential.

XII

THREE CASES

EVERY SCHOOL OF
therapy uses the client's verbal productions as a basis for intervention. Some take client history quite literally. Others use client verbalization as a guide to the discovery of immediate concerns. Two of the clients presented here expressed these concerns in the form of letters to the therapist. The third case is a history of treatment over a three-month period.

The first client, a young woman in her twenties, is married with no children. She writes:

> *I suppose the main problem is almost complete lack of confidence in myself. I'm always unsure of how to act with people—so much so that it causes pain and shaking inside of me. I feel so out of place in just about every situation, and when I do feel comfortable it's such a relief that I try so hard to keep the feeling there that I miss what is really before me. I want so to be liked by everyone so I'm always trying to fit into a new image; one I think the person I'm with will like. So it's not very often that I'm really*

79

me. That's what causes the most hang up of all, knowing who I am, sometimes I feel so close—but one little change from the outside world and I'm confused and uncomfortable. I know I'm not a dumb person but so often I feel this way. I seem to get hold of my feelings and be strong and sometimes it lasts for days or weeks. Then somehow either little things are building up or there's a major change and I fall apart. I always feel like I have to prove myself to be on stage. I find I'm not hearing things people say. I see their mouth move and hear sounds but I'm not really taking in what is being said.

I can't confront even the closest of friends anymore. I just can't relax. I think of a lot I'd like to do for friends like having them over or just stopping by to see them but it just causes the same uncomfortable feelings. It goes so far that I haven't seen a lot of people I like in months and now they have stopped calling because I never really respond.

I'm also terribly jealous of other women whenever John and I are out. I never feel pretty anymore. I feel everyone else is much better. They all have their heads together but I sure don't. I've broken down several times with John trying to explain how I feel and that's why some times I react so negatively. He is patient, but I feel like I'm pushing him away and that he's going to look for someone else. He means it when he says he loves me. I know that, but for some reason I can't accept it completely, I tell him over and over I love him and it hurts so bad inside because I don't feel like I'm really coming across. I anticipate things happening days before—so that when it finally happens I've thought of all the negative thoughts, with a few good ones, that I'm totally upset. Times where I used to have such fun are so hard now —like reading a book—I haven't finished one in about a year. Going out is very hard for me—and now that John's brother is living with us, I find John spends a lot of the time we used to with him. Some of these things—well really most of what I've written down—I'm not sure if I imagine them or they're real—but it becomes so intense that it takes over all reasoning and I become so afraid, and worried, and nervous. John has now noticed it too, more and more. He is trying to help, but I suppose it's that fact that he knows all this that I try so hard to hide, sometimes so

80

much that I just don't talk very much. And I become uptight with his brother around too!

I want so much to be a peaceful person who gives out a lot of love which I have inside—I want to be comfortable with people again—and do silly carefree things. —I want to feel good and at ease walking down the street. I want to like what I am, what I'm wearing and where I am.

I just haven't been able to cope.

Please help me understand some of this so I can begin to live life fully again.

This letter graphically describes the predicament of a person who has no sense of *self*-support. She is oriented toward external support. When she victimizes herself by retroflected condemnation she loses contact with the person she is with. Her uncomfortable feelings result from holding-in breathing and "holding-on" waiting for support that doesn't come. Her difficulty in communicating with her husband demonstrates her inability to distinguish between her projections and his responses. Her letter strongly indicates that her cherished feelings of peacefulness were achieved by an escape into confluence since these feelings disappear when she encounters real contact. She well understands the crux of her dilemma: Knowing who I am. The consequences of her lack of *self*-support are manifested by symptoms of tension, emptiness, depression, depersonalization, withdrawal, and failure. She seeks external support to fill her emptiness, but fears contact which will expose (to her) the pain of her emptiness. Here is the self that fears to be aware of its fear.

In a therapy session she describes an incident in which her car broke down on the way to work and in reporting how she explained the incident to her supervisor she states, "I was so worried that she didn't believe me." The client states that she

81

wants very badly to succeed at her job but feels she should be offering much more than she is.

Although there are undoubtedly issues of omnipotence and authority conflict that might ultimately be dealt with here, the immediate problem was looked at in terms of her need for freedom from a commitment that she felt guilty about. It developed that, although she was now working with developmentally disabled children, her original vocational goal had been to do dance therapy and that her guilt was concerned with her feeling of having betrayed her own potential. She has projected the responsibility for her self-punishment onto others, which has produced the impasse in which she feels trapped. She resents her environment because it does not validate capacities that she is unwilling to express. In existential terms her time is valueless to her because she has nothing to give. A rational approach to her situation would bring out the valuable capacities which she clearly recognizes she does possess. A moral approach could emphasize to her her constructive intentions. The existential approach focusses on her sense that time to-be is eluding her.

For the free individual, time is opportunity. For the prisoner, time is a burden. For the individual securely enmeshed in an environmental support-system, oblivion of time is no problem but, when ego-logic is confronted with silence, the now-present is unendurable. For this client to have to avoid her sense of self makes the present unendurable. For her to decide to turn away from the *self*-oblivion in which she now exists, she must confront the threat that she is avoiding — being in the present. The rational and moral approaches attempt to secure the future by providing time-independent objects for ego to hold on to. In restoring the sense of involvement with the present, the existential approach uncovers the mental structures that would substitute a forever-frozen time for the future reality of change and excitement. To give up these objective guarantees is to recognize and take *self*-iden-

82

tity to heart. The courage to-be appears when the death of these cherished objects is seriously mourned.

The Case of Helen

The following is the case of a young women raised in affluence but emotionally deadened by parental oppression. Led by irrational impulse, she precipitates herself, her husband, parents, and in-laws into a serious crisis. At first she is woodenly immune to feeling pain or understanding the meaning of her act. For Helen, therapy was a process of daring to *accept* acceptance.

Helen, a 21-year-old woman, recently married to a 23-year-old man, is the defendant in a legal case. She grew up with a half brother (6 years her senior) from her mother's first marriage and a younger sister. Her half brother was always rejected by his stepfather and everyone in the family was forced to take sides in the violent conflict that revolved around him. She was isolated and overprotected from childhood. Affection and friendly give-and-take were absent in her family. Parenting was rigidly authoritarian and child-to-parent communication consisted of docile assent to parental values. Corporal punishment was a frequent humiliation even in adolescence. Her brother survived to become autonomous. Her sister is a shy person. Helen adopted the scapegoat role. In this crisis her in-laws are being sympathetic and supportive, both emotionally and financially. Her mother is angry and vituperative. She has not talked to her mother.

In therapy Helen presented a condition of agitation and helplessness with symptoms of phobic hysteria. Her husband was gentle, pleasant, passive, and glad to surrender the leadership in conjoint therapy meetings to her. She had two immediate problems and one long-range problem which were:

1) To cooperate with her attorney and develop support from herself and others in order to present a responsible court-room posture.

83

2) To raise money from her family and in-laws for restitution.

3) To reorient her self-image from that of "abandoned" child hoping for rescue from the label of thief to that of an adult woman able to be responsible for her own life.

As scapegoat Helen's current position is one of considerable power—much more power than she ever enjoyed before. This is the source of her phobic symptoms. She is the object of attention from her employer's attorneys as well as the criminal justice system. She has achieved a position of power with her parents and in-laws that she never had before. Her name has been in the local newspapers. And now she is a client calling on a therapist for relief from the negative feelings that this power has brought her. In therapy she avoids expression of negative feelings. She avoids expressing responsibility for the monumental mess that she has drawn all these others into. She sees her suffering only as a displacement onto others. For herself she only sees her suffering in terms of punishment and self-criticism, which everyone around her wants her to deny.

In six sessions of conjoint treatment Helen and her husband spent their time passively protecting each other. Then they decided she should come in alone. In her first individual session she recalled her childhood Script of playing dangerous Games that she got rescued from. One of these at age 6 was sexual experimentation with her 12-year-old brother. Following this session she worked on resolving a difficult current work relationship and following this she had a dream in which she became angry at her mother and yelled at her in the dream—something that never happened in real life. In a preceding dream she tells a man who is on the outs with his girlfriend, "You can't buy back Janet." In an empty-chair psychodrama with mother she remembers coming in from a date at 3 A.M. at age 17. She is timid and pleading and reports to the therapist, "I was angry with her but we stopped before any strikes were blown [sic]." Helen decided to stop "blowing her lines" and write her mother, a step she had been postponing for six weeks.

84

Helen's father is influential in party politics and she vividly remembers the thrill of passing out literature at political rallies when she was four years old. Helen's fairytale Script was that money and power would protect her from the curse of death in ignominy and poverty. Helen believes that she was also cursed by ugliness, an aesthetic failure. She compensated for this by cleverness, which postponed her maturation. She now has a firm personal commitment to her husband with support from his parents. From this transcendent position she can reclaim her aesthetic and ethical deficits and finish up "old business" with her father and mother. Helen will not go on to live "happily ever after" because she is not living a fairytale Script anymore. She and her husband will have to pay her fine and solve the new problems life brings them without depending on magic.

The Case of Marian

The case of Marian is interesting as an example of a change made by a client resulting from a change of approach by the therapist. Marian was never my client. She appeared at the clinic one evening in a state of agitated depression. She was well known in the clinic for having made several suicidal gestures and other manipulative pleas for rescue. On this occasion I talked to her for half an hour and had her admitted to the ward for self-protection. After she returned home her therapist asked me what I thought about her symptoms and showed me several letters she had written him. I abstracted one of the letters and gave the following analysis to her therapist for his consideration.

The text of her letter is in the left-hand column and my analysis is in the right-hand column. This letter demonstrates the polar relationship of *self*: ego. This letter illustrates borderline psychotic functioning and the solution proposed by the client.

85

I can be in serious trouble if my letter gets away from you. I trust you enough to dare to put things to ink.

Client is saying that she is breaking the secret contract that ego will sup-

My past is a mess I can only hope it does not affect my future.

You mentioned a double image. I'll give it to you if you want it. It scares me. Living with it is a nightmare for me. If you can see it, I'm sure others can too. That fact alone means I'm losing ground to its favor again.

Indians call it Manitou (evil spirit). Psychiatry calls it "schizo." I call it Lee. Lee wants me. The conflict is deadly. It has the power to kill me.

That is why I have to stick it out with you or another doctor all the way.

I can't fight it myself and it can hurt others.

When I cry, that thing is about to be turned loose so I run, I isolate myself. If it turns, I'm the only one it can hurt. I fear it because it's my father's creation. It is filled with all his hate, spite and resentment for me.

Its victim is me. It takes all I have to ward off this thing's domination of me. If by chance I snap and you come face to face with Lee, just remember I'm in there somewhere. I can not talk. I cannot obey. I am trapped. My anger has caused me to pass out. It is a way of protecting others from me as a protection measure for me. Lee is dangerous if unleashed. I've never felt her so ready to take over except the night I overdosed. My father played a big hand that night too. I'm I'm no good according to him. My

press her dangerous *self*-expression. Her past *self*-expression is a liability and a future threat. She would like to disown her historical *self*.

She would like the therapist to be responsible for her disowned *self*. The struggle to suppress *self*-expression is emerging. Loss of ego-control will lead to psychosis.

Client sees *self* as an evil spirit that threatens to overwhelm ego. *Self* is named Lee which could be either male or female.

The therapist is to be an ego-ally.

Inability to protect ego against injury.

Projection of introjected material. The narcissistic wound of *self*.

Depersonalization of ego.

Regression.
Psychosis is better than suicide.

Suicide gets the upper hand over psychosis.

Inability to discriminate between father's ego and own ego — symbiotic attachment.

My incompetence and inadequacies are what Lee feeds on in me. My incredible ability for self punishment is the way Lee gets the upper hand.

Lee wants me. She will not hurt unless provoked. She uses me as her defense against restraint. Hurt me and she gains more ground. Leave me alone and she weakens. If she surfaces while I am in your hands, she could be stopped permanently; however, it could damage me. I'm afraid to face her alone. You are a friend. I may pay a price for what I've just told you.

I know I have to stop the conflict in my mind before it stops me. The question is how? Who will help?

Self-hatred — the narcissistic dilemma.

Me = ego. Ego's duty to defend *self*.

Keep ego strong to control *self* at all costs — . The paranoid position.

Narcissistic death — irreversible psychosis.

The therapist as ego-ally.

The price would be irreversible psychosis.

Who will be my ally in the attempt to reconcile ego with *self* and save my life?

In three weeks Marian made a dramatic change. She stopped being depressed, began to achieve at school, and became a joyous person. The therapist treating her commented as follows:

This analysis of Marian's letter, discriminating between ego and self, *has been instrumental in helping me to get Marian to focus on ego-cooperation with her primitive* self. *As therapist I became a* self-*ally in this task and was able to bypass the ego defenses which were stalemating change. Marian is currently employed and is demonstrating her leadership ability. She is now attending college with outstanding academic performance. She is still having some difficulty in forming personal relationships but integration of her fragmented* self *is showing encouraging progress as demonstrated by her emerging affect.*

The point of this case is that simply changing the therapist's viewpoint from analysis of ego-defenses to encouragement of *self*-expression allowed the client to become functional. Marian and I talked later but we did not discuss the reasons for her change. I believe miracles are better left unexplained.

87

XIII

EXISTENTIAL PRACTICE OF PSYCHOTHERAPY

IN ADDITION TO GES-talt Therapy, which emphasizes responsibility and awareness, and Redecision Therapy, which emphasizes contracts and decision, other methods of therapy also employ existential principles. Paradoxical Intervention was originated by Frankl and expanded by Erickson, Haley, and Frankl. Systems Therapy's interest in polarities is related to Paradoxical Intervention. Moreno's Psychodrama was an early form of group therapy. Wilhelm Reich was one of Perls's teachers and his attention to body-awareness has been continued by existential therapies. Stanley Keleman works largely with body-awareness while Eugene Gendlin's Experiential Therapy works to express the meaning of body feelings. Relaxation and guided-imagery methods are an important adjunct to attaining awareness of body feelings. Reality Therapy works with contracts and responsibility. Rational Emotive Therapy seeks to achieve *meta*-transcendence of aesthetic conflicts. The Client-

Centered Therapy of Carl Rogers originated many of the principles of existential therapy.

Brief Therapy

The principle of paradoxical intention first enunciated by Frankl has been applied and expanded by Bateson, Jackson, Haley, and Satir. Haley (1963) and Watzlawick (1974) have made important contributions to the practice of Brief Therapy which makes much use of paradoxical intention. The following is a case example demonstrating breaking an impasse with paradoxical intention.

> In this example related by John Frykman, a visiting therapist was introduced to a person who had been stubbornly mute ever since admission to the ward. The therapist perceived that a hostile staff had selected a difficult patient for him, and he said, "I can understand your anger at being forced to be in here. You resent being put on display for the benefit of people who are unwilling to listen to you. I just want you to know that I support your refusal to talk 100 percent. I have come all the way from California to visit here, though, and I would consider it a personal favor if you could let me know that you understand my concern for you. I don't want you to say anything. Just move your finger a little bit to let me know that you have heard me." Following this, the therapist continued for a couple of minutes with innocuous remarks. And as he was about to rise to conclude the interview, he placed a hand on his partner's knee and said, "Thank you so much for letting me know that you heard me," and the enraged woman shouted, "I never did any such thing."

In this situation the client's *self*-awareness was so focused on her determination not to communicate by finger movement that she overrode her ego-decision not to talk. Milton Erickson (Haley, 1973) is particularly skillful at getting clients to negotiate their aesthetic and ethical dilemmas.

> *In the treatment of an anorexic girl, Erickson (1979) led her to develop her position that starving herself to death was an act of ethical self-sacrifice and then he proceeded to paralyze this position by telling her that she was the most ungrateful person he had ever met because of her refusal to accept things that were offered to her.*

Erickson's therapy is an example of paradoxical double bind. To have challenged the patient on the basis of his rationality would have allowed her to continue her mission of defiance. But to present the patient with the necessity of justifying her delusion on her own grounds cut the ground out from under her autistic withdrawal.

Polar Systems

This case of marital therapy illustrates the identification of complementary polarities:

> *This is the common complaint of Ted and Carol, the dominant wife and the submissive husband. Along with the principal maladaptive symptoms of this couple, there are the satellite symptoms of the anorgastic wife who finds housework boring and nags her husband to perform better on his job and to show more interest and leadership in family decisions. The sexually frustrated husband is underachieving on his job, looking for adult companionship outside the home and resentful of his wife's monopoly of home authority. In therapy sessions, wife and husband are solicitiously overprotective of each other in ways which subtly expose the other's failure to perform according to expected role models. The therapist is invited to validate and support their efforts to salvage this marriage, which, without help, it is averred, is headed for disaster.* (Edwards, 1978)

They provide a wealth of material illustrating the familiar impasses of See how hard I'm trying, Now I've got you, Martyr, Kick Me, If Only, not to mention It's All Your Fault, which is soon to be aimed at the therapist. The therapist is caught between caring for the welfare of the clients and the wish to avoid being tagged with failing to solve their "problems." The "problem" — they are in unanimous agreement — is that the husband should be more aggressive and the wife more submissive. And they, indeed, maintain the problem would be easily solved "if only" each would adopt the behavior which they believe they so desperately covet. Uppermost among their demands on the therapist's expertise is their expressed need to know "why" they are unable to achieve their goals. They profess to be eager to try anything the therapist will suggest and are, at first, disappointed and later critical of the therapist's failure to present workable solutions to their "problem." As the therapist becomes intimately involved in partnership with this couple he increasingly shares their frustration and despair of not seeing an end to the impasse that is blocking therapy.

The therapist now must consider for himself the prescriptions he thinks might be helpful to the clients. First, there is divorce from the clients (termination of treatment); but divorce is what the clients have come to him to prevent. Second, there is acceptance of impasse (interminable treatment); but the clients may not be willing to add the therapist as a regular "third" in their marital conflicts. The third possibility is dissolution of the double bind in which each sees the other as oppressor and his or her own strengths as liabilities.

Watzlawick (1974) suggests that a first step in this process is to redefine the "problem" to eliminate pursuit of impossible solutions and to focus on real possibilities. The improper definition of the problem may arise from universally applying the cultural dictum that happiness requires the male to be dominant and the female submissive. Obviously, in a world in which half the men are more submissive than the other half and half of the women are more aggressive than the other half, many liaisons will be formed in which the wife is dominant and the husband submissive. If a large proportion of these partnerships were not happily accepting their complementarity, the offices of marital therapists would be deluged with clients. The task, apparently, is to deal with the clients who have failed in their wish to reverse their role positions in conformity with the cultural dictum or now wish to rescind their previous acceptance of conformity.

The next step is to identify the polarities operating in the systems. Polarity is the substance of change and impasse is the result of denial or repression of one half of a polarity. A polarity consists of two complementary opposites which are in tension-equilibrium with each other. Some examples of polarities are, pleasure/pain, dominance/submission, aggressiveness/tenderness. Polarity does not emerge unless there is awareness of both of the complementary opposites in tension with each other. A denial of one side of a polarity and a wish for its opposite is only fantasy and realizes neither side. A great deal of the energy that the clients and therapist maintain is being expended to develop solutions to the "problem" is being used unproductively to repress awareness of the individual's disowned polarities.

In this marital partnership, each person's critic puts him/her into an internal double bind by labeling his/her overt behavior as unacceptable and generating a wish fantasy as a substitute for complementary behavior. The possibility of achieving the wish fantasy is negated by the repression of the behavior that would allow the fantasy to be realized. Hence, frustration.

Harassed by the double bind, which they themselves have generated, each sees the other as the oppressor and his/her own power as the betrayer. This is the external double bind. Systems theory predicts that if one link in the double-bind chain is broken the system will reform more appropriately. For example, if either the wish fantasy or the critic role were abandoned, then the individual's repressed behavior would appear as a true polarity in equilibrium with his/her overt behavior. And, when polarity is manifested, the impasse dissolves.

In Gestalt Therapy this may be demonstrated by asking the client to dramatize his wish fantasy, thereby exposing his critic role (Fagan, 1970). According to Communications Systems Therapy (Watzlawick, 1974), the therapist can tell clients that, truthfully, their disowned overt behavior may not be the way they want the world to see them but they evidently have been born unlucky and they would be better off to resign themselves to failure and to console each other, rather than to continue to exhaust themselves in the effort to rescue the other partner from his/her cruel fate. And, at the same time they must assume the infinitely hard task of making an extra effort to live their own "true" roles, that is, whenever the wife wishes she were tender, she should come on dominant, and whenever the husband wishes he were strong, he should come on tender. This latter instruction focuses attention on the repressed behavior and confuses the "critic."

The therapist's countertransference double bind can be viewed in the same way as that of the clients'. The therapist is frustrated and resentful that the clients are not "taking care of" him and responding to his therapeutic intervention. He feels guilty in response to the clients' rejection and wants their acceptance. The therapist perceives his frustration and anger as unacceptable (to him) and attempts to promote his "capable therapist" wish role. All the while, his repressive critic is sabotaging the real strength that would be available to him if he would express his anger and drop his fantasy-therapist role. The resolution of the double bind for the therapist comes when he/she recognizes the denial and abandons his wish fantasy. The therapist wish fantasy may alternate between dominant/aggressive and tender/submissive, so both examples may apply to the therapist.

If the therapist can model resolution of his double bind, there is a good possibility that the clients will accept this for themselves. Then again, they may become enraged by what they see as a thinly camouflaged deception. And, realizing that they don't need to continue this charade, they quit therapy content with themselves. The therapist always has to risk the possibility that the client will get well in spite of him.

Reality Therapy

The therapies of Glasser and Ellis are directive, problem-solving approaches to treatment. Their thrust is for choice, not insight. In my opinion they provide useful frameworks for treatment planning which, with a richer philosophic orientation by the therapist, can promote authentic *self*-determination by the client. The source of anxiety is ego's attempt to rationalize its contradictory paradoxes that it can never escape. Rational, cognitive therapies divert the attention of client and therapist from the feeling of anxiety to its "causes," but the real need is to control the process, not the "cause" (content).

Reality Therapy (Glasser and Zunin, 1979) rejects the medical model of mental "illness." It focuses on present behavior and concrete plans for changing behavior rather than feelings *about* behavior. It reinforces success rather than exploring pathology. It uses values clarification as a teaching tool. It denies the utility of transference and unconscious motivation but does require that the therapist communicate a caring attitude to the client. In evaluating the client's success in carrying out a contract for planned behavior changes, the therapist accepts no excuses for failure. To do this would be to admit that the client's commitment to change was valueless. But the therapist does not allow the client to indulge in self-blaming for failure. Instead the therapist encourages the client to renew the commitment and update the plan for change. These are the general directions of all existential methods.

A technique which I use occasionally is to play a game of Hearts with the whole family. Hearts is a fairly sophisticated game em-

phasizing cunning play, vindictive retaliation, and even skillful cheating. It is a game for players of all ages and I have played it for many years with great enjoyment. This particular case involved a 12-year-old boy who had an 11-year-old brother and several older sisters. Father and mother were both bright, active people who had a good parental relationship with the children, albeit father was away from home considerably with a highly responsible job. It was clear from the first family session that the girls and boys separated themselves into distinct subgroups.

The problem that brought the family into treatment was that the 12-year-old son had been involved in delinquent acts over the last 3 years and the latest incident, in company with a neighborhood boy, had caused considerable damage. Juvenile Probation and the insurance carrier wanted some assurance of rehabilitation, or drastic measures such as court wardship would be instituted.

Individual interviews with the "identified patient," conjoint interviews with the parents, and meetings with the entire family failed to reveal any symptoms of serious pathology or any clues as to the seat of the child's anger. At this point I scheduled a family Hearts game to be held at home. In this game the two boys chose seats on each side of mother. Father and I occupied spots among the girls. I sat directly across from mother and the boys. When a large group of people play, 104 cards (two decks) are used. This accentuates the competitiveness of the game.

What I observed was that, while the 12-year-old client was a competent and motivated player, his younger brother pretended to be stupid, continually asked mother for help (and received it), and harassed the 12-year-old. When in the course of the game the 12-year-old suffered losses he smarted with humiliation but said nothing. His brother got sympathy and strokes for his misfortunes.

Following this illuminating meeting I met with father and mother and got their agreement for some changes in the way the boys were to be treated.

95

1) The 12-year-old was to have a locked box for his private storage. He was to have exclusive use of selected toys and he was to be taken alone with father for a few special treats during the year.

2) The 12-year-old was to be complimented for his excellent schoolwork and the younger brother was to get special help to get his schoolwork up to par.

3) Shirking, bugging, and "dirty tricks" by the younger brother were not to be tolerated or condoned by mother; and father was to support her in disciplining the younger brother who was "getting away with murder."

Two more sessions were held with the client to explore his feelings of excitement about illegal acts. It was suggested that he pay close attention to the consequences of criminal activity that were portrayed on TV shows that he was allowed to watch. There was no discussion of his relations with his brother nor was there any discussion about the immorality of his actions. This was several years ago and nothing further has been heard from the family or the Probation Department and it is assumed that the client has stopped delinquent activity.

Rational Emotive Therapy

In defining R.E.T., Ellis writes:

When a highly charged emotional consequence (C) follows a significant activating event (A), A may seem to, but actually does not, cause C. Instead, emotional consequences are largely created by B—the individual's belief system. When an undesirable emotional consequence occurs, such as severe anxiety, this can usually be traced to the person's irrational beliefs, and when these beliefs are effectively disputed (at point D), by challenging them rationally, the disturbed consequences disappear and eventually cease to recur. (1979, p. 185)

It appears from this that Ellis looks to remove the cause of anxiety rather than to control its process.

Ellis is cognitive and antideterministic. Following Adler, he rejects the linear Stimulus-Response (S-R) mechanism. Ellis' approach is wholistic and relativistic (dialectical). Ellis actively teaches and conditions the client to explore alternate choices. In his emphasis on *blaming as a prime factor in emo-*

tional disturbance Ellis is in agreement with Rogers, Glasser, Satir, Perls, and Berne. Contrary to Rogers, Ellis actively attacks the client's irrational beliefs, whereas Rogers *understands* the client's need to be irrational. This difference is dramatically portrayed in the film *Three Approaches to Psychotherapy* (Shostrom, 1965) in which Ellis, Rogers and Perls successively interview the same client. In this film Ellis comes on as a benevolent tyrant while Rogers is benign and attentive. I am in disagreement with the idea that the client's fixed beliefs should be actively attacked, but certainly a major focus of treatment in existential therapy is on developing the contradictory bipolar nature of the client's ego-image system. The desired end result of Ellis's attack on the client's ego-omnipotence is the *meta*-shift to *self*-consciousness. Where Ellis and Berne attempt to reach this by cognitive conviction, Perls, for example, would favor dramatic expression.

Psychodrama

Jacob Moreno is responsible for demonstrating the function of psychotherapy as the stage for the manifestation of transcendent *self*hood. Moreno opened his Spontaneity Theater in 1921. Spontaneity and creativity are the foundations of Moreno's therapy. As spontaneity increases, anxiety decreases. In psychodrama there is no transference relationship with a therapist. It is up to the actors to be what they are. Psychodrama promotes the intensity of catharsis and enhances community feeling. It is the forerunner of modern group psychotherapy.

97

Spontaneity is an adequate response to a new situation or a novel response to an old situation. . . . The terrifying thing for an actor is this wavering between a situation which he has just abandoned, and to which he cannot return, and a situation which he must attain in order to get back in balance and feel secure. . . . The actor's (personal) investment in his life situation has taken away his riches — energy, spontaneity, creativity. Psychodrama gives them back to him. When he can be the persons he hallucinates, they lose their power over him and he gains this power for himself. (Sahakian, 1976, p. 489)

Body Therapies

Therapies in which body and mind cooperate to produce self-support are holistic therapies. The biopsychic bases of holistic therapy have been widely explored. Selye (1976) and Seligman (1975) have made important contributions to understanding the effect of stress on behavior. De Ropp (1968) and Simeons (1962) have written two books of general interest on the subject of mind-body functioning. The verdict of the depth therapies agrees with the wisdom of antiquity — the destiny of ego and body is union in identity. For Freud body-consciousness was expressed in dreams. For Jung it was expressed in symbols. Reich believed that the unconscious is the body. Perls, Reich's pupil, said that neurosis was ego's inability to satisfy the body's organismic need for growth. Holistic therapy since Reich (1976) has seen body and psyche as one system. Therapies vary in their method of developing the client's consciousness of this interrelationship. Bioenergetic therapies focus directly on body processes to manifest ego-alienated feelings. Verbal therapies focus on ego's denial of body feeling. The end goal for both is biopsychic identity. Direct body therapies have been developed by various individuals. Major persons listed by Schutz (1979) are Rolf, Feldenkrais, Lowen, Selver, and Alexander. Although the direct body therapies are practiced predominantly by specialists, the verbally oriented holistic therapist needs to be familiar with their principles. More than this, therapists who undertake the risk of an existential relationship with the client need to know how to re-

98

pair their own tissue stresses. For this, personal participation is these treatments is helpful.

Western culture long ago lost contact with the primitive experience of being alive to body-consciousness. Today there are few anthropological bridges between modern ego-consciousness and primitive body-consciousness and it is impossible to translate this primitive experience into academic language. Modern psychotherapy has inherited the legacy of a scientific determinism founded on the Cartesian mind-body duality. The individual comes to psychotherapy experiencing anxiety. The symptoms of anxiety are those of the body in trouble:

1) Conflict between hunger for positive stimuli and the desire for relaxation of undischarged tension. (Agitation)

2) The attempt to maintain control by flight to the impossible and veto of any current action. (Confusion)

3) Immobilization of the organ function which would express the feared dangerous affect. (Depression)

4) Retreat to a regressed identity that is unable to deal with unfinished infantile shame and abandonment situations. (Regression)

Existential therapy teaches ego to hear and understand the message of the body in trouble. Stanley Keleman is an exponent of the life of the body par excellence. He is a philosopher, poet, and prophet of human fulfillment. His books *The Human Ground* (1975) and *Living Your Dying* (1974) should be read by every therapist. One of Keleman's major points is that modern culture stifles human be-ing by substituting mind fantasy for body experience. Therapies that treat ego "problems" instead of human be-ing reinforce rather than heal ego:body alienation. Ego:body integration restores self-support and manifests the experience of body-consciousness that mind fantasy has deadened and distorted. The distortion process leaves its mark on the body in the form of muscle, armoring, postural defect, and somatic disorder.

99

Restoration of ego:body contact is a necessary component of healing. Keleman writes: "If I am in contact with myself I am in contact with the world. The relationship that I have to myself is the relationship I have to my world. . . . The way [my] body is, is the way [I] am. . . . To be unable to live the body's destiny is to be unable to exist freely." (1975, p. 19, 22)

Experiential Therapy

Jung invented the method of Active Imagination. Since then, others, such as Perls, have made this an integral part of their therapy. Gendlin (1978) has developed a procedure which he names Focusing. Focusing develops awareness of the meaning of body-feeling states. The sequential steps of focusing are: a) preparation 1) clearing mental space 2) feeling for the problem 3) finding the crux 4) labeling 5) checking back with the feeling 6) another cycle, 1 through 5.

The recommended preparation is finding a comfortable place, a place where your attention is not claimed by familiar activity, and, if practical, a person to be with.

Clearing mental space is done by generating an attitude of detachment and waiting to see what "felt" problems spontaneously appear. At this point one does not go into the problems but merely lists them mentally. Clearing a space is setting the stage for a *meta*-shift from ego-logic to *self*-consciousness — not consciousness of self-objects (self-image) but awareness of *self*-consciousness.

Feeling for the problem is done by letting body-consciousness react to the listed problems and identifying which one, or ones, generate strong feelings. Again, one must not dissipate the focus on the feelings by ego-analysis and thinking about "solutions."

Finding the crux occurs as the felt sense connected with

the problem emerges from the background and becomes the figure of interest. This is accompanied by a shift of body tension. Ego observing this body-shift now labels the figure of interest that appeared in step 3.

In step 5, ego checks back with *self*-consciousness to confirm that its label fits the feeling and keeps doing this until a perfect match is obtained as confirmed by the body-shift.

In the 6th step the result of the first series is taken and subjected to another cycle of finding a new crux and labeling the new feeling.

If at any point ego takes over with logical analysis, then one returns to step 1 and clears mental space to allow continuation of the focusing process. The key to focusing is practice of achieving distance or detachment from ego-logic:ego-image engagement.

Relaxation Methods

Clearing mental space is facilitated by simple relaxation procedures. Diaphragm breathing is the foundation of all relaxation procedures. Most clients, unless they have had singing lessons, are upper-chest breathers. In diaphragm breathing the upper chest is not expanded and air intake is accomplished by moving the diaphragm up for exhalation and down for inhalation. Learning to move the diaphragm up to exhale is aided if the client is instructed to sit in a chair and push against a wall or other firm object with both hands while inhaling. The arms should be slightly bent at the elbows. The sequence for breathing is: inhale 4 seconds, hold the breath for 2 seconds, exhale for 5 seconds, hold the exhalation for 2 seconds, etc. The client is told that once this breathing pattern is established to omit the 4-2-5-2 counting and count silently on each successive exhalation as follows: Owonn (one), Twooo, Three, Fourrr. On the fifth exhalation the one, two, three, four cycle should be recommenced. This is Le Shan's method (1975).

Massage is helpful, especially for the relaxation of shoulder, neck, and jaw muscles, from which tension and headaches originate. It is helpful to have a partner, but self-massage is equally effective. Many books are available on massage. Simple yoga stretching exercises are useful for relaxing leg, trunk, and back muscles.

Guided Meditation

Meditational practice, autogenic therapy (Luthe, 1969), guided imagery (Masters and Houston, 1972), and relaxation methods are essential ways of attaining *self*-awareness. *Self*-awareness emerges most widely in hypnagogic states when ego-reflective thinking is suspended. Ego-*willing* does not reach *self*-awareness. On the contrary, *self*-awareness emerges as the result of letting go of ego-functioning that interposes reflective thinking between the appearance and reality. The following is a meditational exercise suggested by Stern (1978) that affords one the opportunity of experiencing his fear of death.

1) The reader is asked to remember a profound childhood loss such as the death of a favorite pet.

2) Be this child and fully re-experience this moment.

3) Now attend to your present feelings about the memories which you have rediscovered.

4) Now visualize this child in the room with you.

5) When you have visualized your child, go to meet it, express your present feelings, and listen to the response.

The author's most traumatic childhood experience at six was the administration of anesthetic preceding a tonsillectomy —

an experience of utter terror. In concluding the exercise dealing with this moment, my promise to my child was, "I won't let you die." And my child's response was, "I want to grow up to be like you."

In moments of horrible terror when the sense of flow-of-time is stopped to avert the imminent realization of a terrifying occurence, time collapses and ego is unable to go on. The occurence happens inexorably but ego never admits the wound which *self* has experienced. For ego to recover wholeness of life is to be able to forgive *self*-wounding. The sacred art of therapy is to be able to participate in this service of Caring.

Client-Centered Therapy

For a recent issue of *Voices* (1978), the journal of the American Academy of Psychotherapists, the editorial advisors were asked to respond to the question: Who in your opinion is the therapist, now living, who has made the greatest contribution to psychotherapy? The one who received the most mention was Carl Rogers. Carl Rogers, more than any other individual, has identified and fought for professional recognition of the necessity for a transcendent personal relationship between therapist and client. Rogers's principles of Client-Centered Therapy are (Rogers, 1966):

1) That the therapist is in an egalitarian partnership with the client.

2) The therapist does not invade the client's privacy uninvited, with interpretations, advice, and judgments.

3) The focus of therapy is on the client's awareness of his phenomenal world.

103

4) The art of the therapist is the ability to develop an empathic sharing of experience with the client.

5) Therapeutic intervention is directed by the client's choice of goals for behavioral change.

The client assumes the responsibility for undertaking these changes and the therapist agrees to assist. The work of therapy is overcoming the obstacles which arise between client and therapist in their attempt to carry out this contract. The end of therapy is that clients are able to ask for, and negotiate with others, for what they want.

This chapter has presented some existential aspects of several therapeutic methods. Existential method is focused on ways of being: spontaneity, awareness, responsibility, caring. Its method is action, rather than cognitively, directed. Its method is to transcend impasses in the service of consummating the possibilities of client-defined goals. It would be a mistake to read this chapter as an exposition of various therapeutic techniques that might be used as a method of therapy. Existential therapy, no less than any other practice, imposes the obligation on the therapist to be *there* to the client. For the therapist to be able to meet this obligation requires disciplined practice of his *self*-revelation of be-ing.

XIV

THE REDEMPTIVE COMMUNITY

Group Therapy

THE CONTEMPORARY practice of group therapy is the fruition of the application of existential principles. For a therapy that stops trying to explain *why* the client chooses his behavior and looks at *how* he expresses himself, group therapy is the arena of action. In this arena the therapist is not the passive observer waiting to analyze events as they spontaneously emerge. For the existential therapist, group therapy represents an opportunity for the members, including the therapist, to discover *self*hood in person-to-person contact. The therapist is actively engaged with the client, giving unequivocal messages, expressing his need for response, and projecting his *self*-consciousness.

The elements of activity that characterize the work of many group therapists can be grasped from the following list of "rules" which distinguish existential therapy from interpretive therapy.

1) *Why* questions are out of order. No one is allowed to be Mr. District Attorney. Why questions are rephrased as *I* statements.

2) One is not allowed to speak-for other persons or discuss them in the third person as though they were not in the room.

3) Game "payoffs" that are inflicted on others or on oneself are reframed rather than reinforced. "Reframing" is a strategy named by Watzlawick (1974, 1978) and also by Satir (1964, 1972). The four books by these authors are the most helpful books for teaching therapists that I know of.

4) Group members are told that they can talk when they wish to and remain silent when they wish to and that the therapist will not invade their privacy. They do not need "permission" to leave the room.

5) Statements that imply that some person or some "thing" *makes* a person have a feeling are mildly challenged. There are no "its" making people have feelings.

6) Careful distinctions are made between "thinking" and "feeling." The purpose of therapy is to train the individual to be aware of what he *feels*, cognizant of what he *thinks*, and responsible for action that he decides to undertake in-the-now.

7) The therapist states that he will express his wishes and expects others to do the same. "Mind-reading" is not practiced and if one wishes the therapist to stop working with him, a simple request is sufficient.

8) One is not allowed to pretend that an unintelligible or double-bind message makes sense.

9) "War stories" and out-of-the-room anamneses are not a ticket of admission to group therapy. Likewise, "entertaining" displays of pseudo-feeling are not rewarded with applause. This mission of group therapy is to teach its members to enjoy each other, not torture them.

10) The client contract is essential to therapy. The contract consists of what the client expects to achieve and how he will know when he has achieved his goal. Contracts to gain "more self-confidence" are no good. The client must state what having more self-confidence will let him do that he cannot do now.

11) The therapy group is not a committee to assess blame, hear excuses, or give advice. Each client comes as an individual to do his or her own work. The therapist can choose to work with whoever wishes his service.

Of the twelve schools of therapy discussed by Corsini (1979), six are practiced largely in group settings. Schutz (1979) has named some forerunners of therapy groups. Among these are: the Greek drama, Mesmer's groups, pietistic religious movements such as Hassidism and Methodism, and Stanislavski in the theatre. In the field of psychotherapy, group therapy and the therapeutic milieu represent the effort to translate one-to-one transference into group commitment. Encounter groups, N.T.L. training groups, marathon groups, and all kinds of "growth" groups seek to effect personal change through group commitment. The therapeutic community extends this concept to residential and/or long-term community programs. Many secular movements are successful in invoking passionate personal commitment, albeit, they demand varying degrees of personal responsibility. Examples of these range all the way from Walden II to Jonestown. The more limited the personal responsibility, the less humane the behavior of the group members.

A prime principle of the therapeutic community is individual responsibility for choice. One is responsible for the action that is done as well as for what is not done—for need that is expressed and for the expression of need that is withheld. One is responsible for experiencing being responsible. Sartre put it thus: I cannot be vulgar except in the presence of the Other (1965, p. 188). The therapeutic group focuses on and augments one's experience of being experienced. One

107

becomes aware of oneself both as manifester and experiencer. This is in contrast to avoidance procedures such as projection and confluence. In projection one attempts to get others to take responsibility for one's own self-conceived absolutes. In confluence one attempts to avoid responsibility for delegating *self*-awareness to others — or to some transcendent universal. Either of these movements results in a loss of contact and authenticity. As an example of projection, group members who fail to get strokes for dominating the group play Poor Me. For this they get kicked by the group and this validates the projection that people are hostile. In the case of confluence, one wants to be accepted but is unwilling to express this out-front. Instead, the group member expects the group to guess what is wanted and then plays Poor Me when the others refuse to guess. Another example of projection and confluence is "talking-about" or Ain't it Awful. The confluent group merges into inauthenticity and by group consensus constitutes an imaginary absolute to validate their prejudices. Psychodynamic transference encourages the development of inauthentic behaviors so that they can be interpreted to the client. Existential therapy does not accept transference and offers the client the experience of the behavior instead of an interpretation.

One of the most informative descriptions of the practice of group therapy is provided by Mary and Robert Goulding in their book, *Changing Lives Through Redecision Therapy* (1979). Their practice is based on Transactional Analysis and Gestalt Therapy. The content of the book deals with the elements of the Gouldings' therapy system: contracts, stroking, impasses, redecisions, and emotions. The transcripts of therapy sessions convey the enthusiasm, spontaneity, and directness of their practice. In the spirit also expressed by Watzlawick and Satir they demonstrate how clients contact and manifest *self*-support and decide to give up unrewarding coping strategies.

The following cases are examples of client work done in the author's groups.

Jack was profoundly depressed because things were going wrong at work over which he had no control. He related to the group one night that he had spent the previous night in a local motel with a loaded shotgun at his head. He came to the group to tell them that he had decided not to pull the trigger. He decided that he was not responsible for the whole world. A few weeks later he called the therapist to say he was discontinuing the group because he was going to lodge meeting on that night. He related that he had stopped being depressed and wanted the therapist to convey his thanks to the group for their support. He has had no recurrence of depression.

This case is an example of Gestalt dream work. A woman married to an alcoholic husband was hooked into the classic "rescue" game played by spouses of alcoholics. In a group meeting she enacted a Gestalt psychodrama of a dream in which her dead mother fell through the ice and she was unable to rescue her. Her work ended with saying goodbye to mother. Following this meeting she decided to go back to school and become independent of her husband's problems. He has been sober now for two years.

In the following case a woman who had been repeatedly hospitalized for manic episodes, even while being maintained on lithium medication, achieved control as a result of being stroked for good performance. She has not been back to the hospital for three years in spite of several traumatic family crises. She joined with another formerly nonachieving group member to use her experience in a day treatment group for chronically disturbed outpatients and has discontinued lithium medication.

This case is an example of the results of training a client to make contact with straight messages. Al was involved in a heavy Game of Kick Me with his wife of eighteen years. The game culminated one night when he consented to go with his wife to seek voluntary admission to the psych ward. His wife saw this as a last-ditch effort to cure Al of his passive/aggressive behavior and Al saw it as a last-ditch effort to get away from his wife without his having to make the decision. The admitting doctor disappointed them both, however, and Al was referred to the outpatient clinic. Al spent several weeks avoiding contact with his therapist by reciting the history of his unsatisfactory marriage

109

and the therapist sent him in desperation to group therapy. The group gave Al no strokes for playing Kick Me but listened when he made in-the-room contact. In a few weeks Al reported that his rancorous arguments with his boss had ceased and he was being considered for promotion. His wife decided that if therapy could change Al that much, she would go to see a therapist. She was referred to one who specialized in avoiding "bear trappers." Al's wife had left family therapy in a flying rage when challenged by one of her sons. After several more months Al has decided he has received maximum benefit from the group and has joined Alcoholic's Anonymous. This mystified the therapist since neither Al nor his wife had ever suggested that he had a drinking problem.

In this case, the client's game was See How Hard I'm Trying. Predictably, she was afflicted with severe chronic colitis. She arrived one night to find a note on the office door saying that the therapist had gone home ill and regretted not being able to inform all the members in time. She reported the following week that she had been angry at being "stood up" by the therapist, and had said, Gestalt fashion, to the closed door, "Well if that's all you care about me, I can take care of myself." As she reported at the next meeting, she went home and took her vitamins and her colitis has never returned. She quit lamenting about being left by her "loser" husband and is now happily married. She also found herself a stimulating job.

Cora's Game in the group is to pass out Rescue Stamps. One night she wondered out loud in group why her welfare checks were always late. A group member who sometimes plays straight man for Cora said, "I bet you forgot to send in your income report." "Oh yes," said Cora, "I write it out, put it in an envelope and stamp it and then I leave it in my purse." Turning to the group leader she said, "Why do I do that?" The group leader responded, "Next month, throw it in the toilet." Shocked, Cora said, "Well, if I do that I can't send it to Sacramento." "Yes, but I'll bet you don't put it in your purse," replied the group leader.

110

In my groups I am a nondirective leader. There are rarely any dramatic explosions or searing revelations. Individuals get stroked for transcending their problems by being in-the-room. They learn to get support by giving strokes, asking for strokes, and accepting strokes. They learn to care for one another and to love themselves. I have learned in these and many other cases to have faith in the redemptive power of the unexpected.

Communal Groups

Two groups that have extended the principle of group therapy to communal living are The *Family* (Edwards, 1973) and Synanon (Simon, 1978). I have had first-hand experience in both of these communities.

Synanon was begun by Dederich in 1958 and The *Family* was begun by Garrigues in 1968. Both of these communities were formed to rehabilitate drug addicts and are organized around the **Game.** The **Game** is a type of marathon encounter group. Where Simkin (1974) and Goulding, for example, may conduct four-week live-in training groups, which are in effect ongoing marathons, the **Game** is the basis of a continuing encounter community. The Lake Cowichan Gestalt community of Perls (1975) is a continuing encounter community conducted according to the principles of Gestalt Therapy. The existential principle followed in these groups is that the responsibility to oneself supercedes every other concern. At the time of this writing (1979), the founder of Synanon, Charles Dederich, is the subject of considerable controversy and the outcome of his case is uncertain. I believe, however, that whatever Dederich's individual fate, the teaching of personal commitment furnished to Synanon community members will persevere.

The early career of the potential drug user begins, as does that of most persons whose manifest emotional disorder persists to adult life, with ambivalent, ambiguous, and inconsistent parenting. From his earliest memory, rational thinking

111

by the child is discounted by his parents and emotional rewards are inappropriate and lacking. Between the ages of four and six the child's innate potential for reality testing begins to assert itself and the child occasionally demands rational, appropriate responses from his parents. Failing in this demand, he makes two important decisions. First, he abandons efforts at rational behavior and his impulse control becomes fixated at his four-year-old level; and, second, he decides to reject the real existence of his natural parents (Spiegel, 1959).

This produces a homeless four-year-old wanderer who has decided to spend his life looking for mythical parents to legitimate his existence. He searches for mythical parents and tests those he meets to see if they will qualify themselves as mythical parents. He thereby creates transference, rather than real, relationships with significant others such as friends, teachers, bosses, and spouses. The urgency of the child-victim's quest originates in his death-wish, which he has formulated in the statement directed to his parents: "You will know that I am your child when I die." Thus the death-wish is not a gross manipulative appeal for general social approval but a crucial existential test directed toward forcing a particular father and a particular mother to recognize the unique identity of their child. Since these particular parents did not, do not, and probably will not ratify this request, the child-victim is doomed to a frustrating odyssey in which all potential parents turn out to be strangers who attack him.

The therapeutic solution carried out in the **Game** is to reveal and control the fixated child now living in an adult body and to train the adult to recognize and relate to real people. When he is able to do this, his four-year-old child is now able to know that he really was the offspring of his natural parents and to see himself as a real person. When he can see the real identities of his father and mother he no longer has to clothe others with fictitious masks nor shield himself with a magic mask. The keystone of the **Game** is uniform opposition to the transference demand. This opposition is consistently presented in the message "We are your teachers, not your parents, and when you stop testing us as imaginary parents you will become aware of who you really are." In every encounter, every transaction, and every task, the virtue of awareness is transmitted by **Game** members to each other. This is in the service of the member's commitment to pursue life rather than immediate and personal death (by drugs). In the **Game** all spurious loyalties are abandoned, all false roles are revealed, and the individual comes to know who he is. He no longer exhausts himself in useless defenses and is able to enjoy truthful *self*-expression. This is in contrast to the addict's street behavior where stealing was O.K. because nothing had any value, lies were O.K. because guilt had no meaning, and death was O.K. because you couldn't feel it anyway.

The **Game** is the nonviolent equivalent of the wartime battlefield. The **Game** members are drawn by their discipline into a close-knit mutually supporting group. Not only is expression of their daily social frictions frustrated but also their accumulated childhood rage is still repressed. The **Game** is the battlefield where the enemy is attacked. The teaching of the **Game** is that the individual's accumulated rage over real and imagined injustice is both rationally useless to him as well as a barrier to his emotional growth because it prevents him from enjoying excitement which he formerly equated with violence. On a more profound existential basis, the **Game** player undergoes his fantasied death ("I could have died of shame") and finds that he is the last one to recognize what he has been concealing from himself but no one else. This is an essential development in the process of *self*-recognition.

The **Game** has no counterpart in any other system of therapy in that it is an ongoing function of a mutually committed communal group. It is not employed as an arena for therapeutic life-decisions or for producing heightened emotional experience, although these may be incidental to its action. The **Game** starts with an Indictment or Probe of the person in the "hot seat." Other members of the **Game** are expected to support and amplify the Probe. Various techniques are used to exaggerate the impact of the Probe on the person in the "hot seat" and on the other **Game** members. The person in the "hot seat" may respond with a spectrum of behavior ranging from abject silence to frantic verbalization as well as rational defense. Other players may take the "hot seat" away from him. The **Game** is the stage for the acting out of the exaggerated and unreal fantasies of the fixated Child. It is inconsequential whether the positions and emotions of the **Game** players and provocateurs bear any relation to reality, justice, or mercy.

The activity of the **Game** uses the confrontation of the sensitivity group and it uses the primitive explosion of Perlsian Gestalt technique (Perls, 1969). The **Game** has its own unique quality of creative spitefulness. The **Game** depends greatly on light and quick-moving repartee to be effective. **Games** which get involved in "therapeutic" analysis—Hunting For the Easter Eggs—and bog down in ponderous and slow-moving inquiry accomplish nothing except to promote the pathology of the player who is able to control the **Game** in this manner. The **Game** is not intended to give strokes, either positive or negative, to anyone. Since no **Game** player need appear as a real person, the individual is left to his own resources to decide to what extent he has been able to look at his own real *self*.

Simon (1978) points out, however, that what one is responsible for in the **Game** is the polar opposite of what one is responsible for on the "floor" (i.e., life outside of the **Game**). In the **Game** one is responsible for free expression of feelings. On the "floor" one is responsible for ethical behavior. Aesthetic despair is relieved in the **Game** and the ethical part of life is not given the unrewarding task of compensating for aesthetic failure. Schutz's (1979) approach to personal growth puts heavy emphasis on the repair of aesthetic failure by body therapy and nonverbal encounter techniques. Perls (1969), on the other hand, sensed an avoidance of responsibility and denounced the "turners on," calling for cognitive integration of decisions to change.

It is a common experience of those who participate in marathons, workshops and training sessions extending for periods of 48 hours or longer that the euphoric "high" that they acquire wears off following the disbanding of the group. The sense of unique *self*-identity that they possessed as group members also dissipates as they merge into the conformity of life-on-the-street. Many members of the close-knit communities are firm in their determination never to leave the community for life-on-the-street and it is, indeed, a question of how compatible *self*-transcendence is with life-on-the-street. As one group member said rather revealingly, "I feel that I will be tempted to want to live on a higher plane of commitment than I can get others to accept outside the group. Then therapy will have put me in a worse trap than I am in now. I don't want to promise myself something I cannot have."

This is the key question for the existential therapist: How can the therapeutic experience of *self*-transcendence be lived in everyday life? If the existential therapist cannot deal with this problem, then it is safer to offer the client cognitive learning and deterministic therapies. To maintain the personal commitment of the redemptive community in a world where anonymous conformity is the chief refuge from demonic attack requires that one risk being faithful to an experience of personal commitment that may never again be recognized or returned by a person other than the therapist. So the task of the individual who has experienced the curative power of transcendent liberation is to leave formal therapy and set about generating or finding another redemptive community to belong to. That is not a task to be undertaken lightly.

XV

COMMUNITY
MENTAL HEALTH

THE PRACTICE OF IN-
dividual psychotherapy as it started with Freud was an esoter-
ic branch of allopathic medicine. The community mental
health movement which started in the 1950s as a method of
extending the benefits of medical psychiatry to those who
could not afford private fees has now become an instrument
of social policy.

For the last 100 years the state hospital has removed from
the community every unmanageable individual who did not
come under the jurisdiction of the criminal justice system.
Now this is no longer possible and the community mental
health system is expected to negotiate differences between the
expectations of the community and demands of its members
who feel unjustly treated. As other forms of social control —
from the nuclear family to the criminal justice system — become less and less restrictive, the mental health system is being looked to as an agent of expedient persuasion. The mental

health professional is being asked to employ psychiatric expertise to justify misbehavior ranging from premeditated murder to passive refusal to meet the minimum requirements of self-sufficiency.

Two factors have combined to promote the community mental health movement: first, the tenfold increase in the cost of hospital care, and second, the discovery of drugs for the relief of psychotic symptoms. In the last ten years, California state hospital bed capacity for mentally disabled patients has been reduced from over 40,000 to less than 5,000. Other states have followed suit. When a skeptical newspaper reporter asked a county director whether he thought the community mental health system could last without state hospitals, he replied, "It's got to. It's the only thing we have." Now persons who formerly would have spent long periods hallucinating in state hospitals are returned to care facilities in the community and maintained on antipsychotic drugs. Although their hallucinations are relieved, their isolation from social contact is a problem that has only been partially addressed.

A major part of the responsibility for the operation of the community mental health system has been delegated to clinical social workers. The clinical social worker, along with the other professionals in the community mental health system, has a threefold commitment: to organize a preventive community effort, to be an effective advocate for the rights of the client, and to be an ethical and competent therapist. The principal function of social work has always been to administer the provision of community resources to the individual client. The social worker's expertise combines knowledge of both governmental regulations and human behavior. As the social welfare system has replaced individualized budgets with standard grants, its need for highly trained social workers has drastically decreased. The principal interface of the welfare system with the individual is now the eligibility worker and the postal service that delivers his check. Protective service is only provided on request.

Granted that it was a sensible move to relieve the social worker of the task of preparing family budgets, the transition has raised a bureaucratic barrier to helping the client with personal problems. The community mental health system helps to fill that unmet need. With the relaxation of juvenile and family law, issues of misbehavior which were once solved by legal fiat now become matters for voluntary negotiation between the client and the police, the school, his or her close others, and the neighbors. The clinical social worker is a key person in a process that may lead to either reconciliation or separation. The problems presented by addictions, irrational destructiveness, cognitive dysfunction, and social passivity that stem from personality disorders have formed a need for treatment that goes beyond the generation of ego-insight.

The government of Great Britain is so concerned with the social consequences of noncoping behavior that they have appropriated 1.5 million pounds sterling (£1,500,000) to study the sociological causes of emotional depression. At a recent conference on coping with stress, Seligman (1979) stated that up to 40 percent of children studied by him in grades 4 through 6 demonstrated a sufficient degree of depression to account for their below-standard academic performance and behavior management problems. Furthermore, he stated, every depressed child has a depressed mother.

Education and organization of community efforts for the prevention of mental illness are major tasks for clinical social work. The principal characteristics of individuals at risk of mental disability are: 1) No close other who responds to requests for help 2) Abnormal incidence of somatic illnesses 3) Unstable work or social performance 4) Behavioral difficulty resulting from use of alcohol or drugs 5) Retreat from sources of help.

118

In a period of high mobility, absence of the extended family, and disrupted nuclear families, a major preventive effort claiming the attention of clinical social workers is the organizing and fostering of community social networks that intercept persons at risk and also provide supportive help for postcrisis rehabilitation. While the clinical social worker in a public agency has the commission for initiating community organization effort, securing funding is an arduous and time-consuming task. Not just new funding, but even the maintenance of continuing funding requires tedious documentation and extensive reporting in the name of accountability. The real danger to viable community mental health services is that administrative, clinical, and community organization expertise will be compartmentalized and that activity with clients and community will be regulated by push-button response to legislative fiat swayed by the latest pressure group to descend on the state capital. The *necessity* of reconciling this fact with one's therapeutic commitment is an existential problem.

Social work's historical antecedent, voluntary charity, drew its inspiration from religious faith. Existential psychotherapy springs from the philosophy that the ultimate fulfillment of human be-ing is the spiritual bond between individuals. Existential psychotherapy is based on the principle that deep change in a person arises from the impact of the therapist's humanity on the client. Existential philosophy shows how irrational spontaneity that transcends ego-reflection can be a source of healing instead of a weapon of demonic aggression. The therapist who would be an instrument of spiritual healing needs an awareness of transcendent *self*hood that is the ground of his human be-ing.

In the almost fifty years since the enactment of the Social Security Act of 1935, the welfare system has become an instrument of national policy second only to the defense effort. The imminent formation of a national health system will further incorporate the helping professions into the political establishment. The enterprise of clinical social work in this movement is to validate a compassionate heritage that goes beyond the limits of the bureaucratic political structure.

119

The practice of community mental health can have two goals: first, to maintain and reinforce moral behavior, and, second, to help the individual survive tragedy. In planning and promoting a mental health program it is important to distinguish between these two goals. Every member of the community lives at some level of morality. Fewer members of a community recognize a tragic sense of life. Moreover, the individual who feels cheated and betrayed by the social order is frequently a threat to moral conformity. Many members of the moral majority would be quick to declare that to possess a sense of tragedy was an illness per se.

High tragedy can be ennobling and inspiring in literature, in church, on the stage, and even in the therapy meeting. In the press and in the courtroom public opinion misunderstands it miserably. The mission of the community mental health program is to minimize the disruption of personal tragedy to public life. The private practitioner is somewhat protected from the rebellion of the client by inaccessibility to public opinion. Flagrantly immoral behavior on the part of the therapist is generally punished by licensing bodies and occasionally in the courts. Public employees do not enjoy the same protection. They are answerable to advisory boards, grand juries, legislative bodies, and a host of officials ready to respond to the complaints of dissatisfied citizens.

The public enjoys tragic drama as long as it can be confined to the stage or TV screen. It is ashamed when tragedy escapes into public life and its wrath is visited on the one who has failed to shield the community from real contact with tragedy. The commission of community mental health is to solve the client's problem before it becomes a public outrage. Unfortunately for the therapist, it is sometimes the case that the client and the significant others are purposefully seeking a public platform from which to discharge their indignation. At this point the community reacts like a troubled family. The blamers, the placaters, the persecutors, the rescuers and the victims come forth with declarations of self-righteous innocence. Then the community mental health practitioner realizes that one speaks not only to the client, in the privacy of the mental health office, but also to the probation officer, the school counselor, the parent's attorney, the minister, the foreman of the Grand Jury, and the reporters for the press, none of whom may be particularly sensitive to or concerned with matters of psychodynamic principle, the delicacies of transference, or questions of client confidentiality.

A child confesses to her therapist that she has been the victim of sexual abuse. The therapist attempts to get the mother to confirm this. Whereupon the child denies she ever said it and the mother threatens to sue the therapist. The child learns from this that society operates to protect adults, not children, and that therapists are really powerless.

A client reported that her spouse constantly threatened her with a gun and the client was torn between asking for police help and fear of the spouse's retaliation. The therapist told the client that he intended to report this to the police and let them handle it. The peace officer went to the house and told the client he wanted the gun. When the client asked him what to tell the spouse, he said, "Tell him to come down and see me."

A citizen came to the office and stated that one of his friends was making some alarming threats. The therapist, knowing the individual and the kind of threats the person was accustomed to make, replied that if he was about to tell him that his friend was threatening to kill someone, he would have to inform the police. The citizen replied that on second thought he would handle the matter himself. The outcome of his further talk with the person was that he stopped drinking and making homicidal threats — an outcome that the therapist had been unable to achieve with the individual.

121

A client with a long history of revolving-door hospitalizations moved to the community and resumed a pattern of hysterical acting out and overdosing on medication. After three acute hospitalizations the client was told that the next incident could lead to court placement in a long-term care facility. Following this the person became a cooperative outpatient and has suffered no further attacks.

A compensated chronic schizophrenic living in the community on an outpatient basis was being regularly picked up and charged with drunkenness. Investigation by the therapist convinced him that the client was not drinking but was engaged in a Cop-and-Robber game with the officer. The therapist dealt with the situation by going to the officer's Lieutenant and explaining that the client was on psychotropic medication and had been forbidden to drink and that it was important to discover whether his provocative behavior was due to intoxication or decompensation. And, therefore, that the next time the client was arrested he should immediately be given an alcohol breath test. The client was never arrested again.

A client, who, in spite of all therapeutic efforts, regressed to violent paranoid behavior, had been placed in a maximum security institution on court conservatorship. When the conservatorship came up for renewal, the client requested a jury trial to establish the right to be released. This required that two psychiatrists, representatives of the state hospital, and peace officers who had observed the person's recent behavior spend a half-day testifying in court to compel the continuation of treatment.

As a public agency, a mental health service must secure annual approval and appropriation of funds for its future program through a chain of advisory committees and governing bodies. The proceedings before these bodies are open to the public and reported by the press. Equally, it must submit an annual account of its past activity to investigative agencies such as the county grand jury and state and county auditors. A request for augmentation of services is sure to be challenged at many points along the way, and to defend the need for new services always invites the question as to why any services are needed at all.

122

Community mental health is the organized effort constituted and regulated by public authority to control the incidence of mental and emotional disability. It is an ethically sanctioned effort to improve the quality of life for the population at risk, their families, and the community at large. The community is part of the client system and the functions of all its social agencies are coordinated in this effort.

The depth psychology of Freud and Jung is a legacy of the 300-year era of cultural and political development that ended with World War I. The prevailing more of that age was that progress was an inevitable evolutionary process toward a moralistic ideal. Spiritual transcendence and tragic sacrifice were, at best, romantic nonsense and, at worst, a threat to the public order and tranquility. The existential view of human nature is as old as Socrates, but its modern application dates from Kierkegaard and Nietzsche, who were hardly read or understood by anybody writing in the fields of health and psychology before 1940. Rank, Adler, Horney, and Reich were seminal influences for the growth of humanistic psychotherapy, which is now building on existential bases. The existential view of life is that change is the result of personal decision, that progress is not automatic, and that success is learning to survive one's own mistakes as well as the uncontrolled buffetings of society.

XVI

THE DESTINY OF *SELF*HOOD

M A N I S T H E B E I N G
who is a problem to himself.* He is a problem to himself because he knows that he is trapped in the flow of time. His temporal existence is threatened by unpredictable natural catas-
trophes—flood, fire, earthquake, drought. He must struggle
continually against hostile creatures ranging in size from invisible microorganisms to ponderous wild beasts, not to mention his most deadly antagonists, other humans. And, as
though he lacked enemies, man has increasingly become the
victim of the waste products of his own rapacity. The human
race has survived all these forces by learning to transcend the
flow of time. Man's adaptability is based on the belief in timeless, transcendent truth and humans look to this ideal to re-
deem them from the fates that have overtaken other species.

*The term *man* is used here to distinguish the human species from other biological
forms.

In most of their characteristics, contemporary humans are as unrecognizable to their predecessors of A.D. 1200 or 500 B.C. as we will be to our successors of A.D. 2500. Yet in our concern for strategies for transcending the flow of time there is a common drive and a common anxiety. Acceptance of the flow of time is the certainty of inevitable death — one's individual death, the death of the civilization, the death of the human species, and, finally, the death of the planet, which is to become a cold, lifeless cinder in frigid interstellar space. Man is the being who lives as though this will never happen. (Lichtenstein, 1975). History is the record of his self-conceit.

Historically human beings have been classified by the strategies they have adopted for the appropriation of eternal truth. (Coan, 1977, Rychlak, 1977, Niebuhr, 1949) Beliefs in transcendence are defined by the polarities — idealism:naturalism or rationalism:romanticism. All of these concepts postulate the existence of universal models for the providence of humanity. Even before the Greeks, human beings struggled to validate their pretensions to universality. The Greek tragedy depicted the failure of this effort. The Christian church believed that spiritual eternity transcended human temporality. The Renaissance ushered in the timeless infinity of mathematics. The laws of motion derived by Galileo, Kepler, and Newton revealed a world of indestructible matter, energy, and space. Processes could be calculated to move forward or backward at will and the choiceless, valueless, predictable universe came into being. The Fathers of the Holy Office were under no illusions when they foresaw that noetic spirituality would have no place in this world. The world of science produced the industrial revolution, followed by political and economic revolution. Political man endeavored to insure his destiny by the guarantee of political rights for the individual. The economic man of Karl Marx and Adam Smith believed that his transcendent destiny was to conform to the inexorable workings of economic processes.

The evidence that human beings are a problem to themselves emerges when the utopian strategies that they construct to insure their security are overturned by *self*-transcendence. The same capacity that enables them to construct Utopias inevitably leads them to destroy them. Toynbee calls these abortive movements in the disintegration of civilizations "schism in the soul." He writes:

> Our inquiries into the nature and working of Futurism and Archaism have now led us to the conclusion that neither of these two ways of life is permanently *viable* and that the failure of both of them is accounted for by the same fatal error. They are both doomed to fail because both are attempts to perform the impossible acrobatic feat of escaping the present without rising above the spiritual plane of mundane life on Earth. (Toynbee, 1939, p. 132)

Simply put, Archaism is the attempt to regain a lost Garden of Eden and Futurism is the attempt to leap into a future Paradise. Both of these subjects are current best sellers on TV, screen, and paperback racks.

The essence of history is that all attempts to maintain states of suspended time-flow fall before *self*-transcendence. The promise of a heavenly Other World was abandoned in favor of the immediacy of scientific experiment. The vision of a mechanically synchronized universe was overcome by Einsteinian relativity. The ideal of socialist liberation succumbs to the violence of bloody combat. All utopian systems of security are destroyed by the inevitability of existential choice. A freedom obtained by the imaginary suspension of time is unreal. As soon as one attempts to put it into effect, choices and decisions are required. Choice brings one back to the Present and the finality of the guillotine and the cyanide. The paradox of freedom achieved by suspension of choice is that this freedom vanishes as soon as choice is required. The cultural shock manifested when these systems collapse reveals the magnitude of society's investment in the security of choicelessness (Toffler, 1970). The damage to man's anthropocentric primacy from the "Copernican" revolutions of Darwin, Freud, and Einstein was only superficial. The real casualties of these encounters were the systems of time-suspension which they replaced. Repair crews were, however, promptly dispatched and new systems shortly appeared, under other names, of course. A current example is *The Tao of Physics* (Capra, 1977), which confidently proclaims that relativistic physics has now abolished human time. The mark of a really transcendent idea, like this, is that it is even beyond the realm of error. This does not, however, qualify it as truth.[4] The existential view of history is that human beings owe their adaptive survival to the ability to transcend the flow of time, but that through this same transcendence they continually invalidate the truths they invent. All time-independent truths are tested by the exigency of choice. Choice manifests the Present and "makes" history. The freedom in which choice is exercised vanishes, as choice is made, ever to reappear as the opportunity for risking new choices. What history produces is a pattern of dialectical polarities — truth and error, rationalism and romanticism, idealism and naturalism. The attempt to achieve security by obliterating the dichotomy violates the flow of time and kills freedom.

Basic to the principle of a mathematically lawful universe is the assumption of the conservation of mass-energy and the constancy of the velocity of light. It is not that there is any way of proving these assumptions. It is simply that our conservative mathematics would be useless if equations did not balance. These assumptions explain why we are able to carry out the experiments that are successful; they do not account for failure nor do they guarantee the existence of a lawfully ordered universe. Einstein once remarked that "God does not play dice with the universe," and Bohr replied, "Einstein, stop telling God what to do" (Bronowski, 1973).

In Verdi's *Otello,* Iago sings, "I believe man to be the sport of an unjust fate from the germ of the cradle to the worm of the grave. After all this mockery comes Death. And then? death is nothingness." Man's tragedy is that he will never know whether the dice are loaded. His glory is that he decides to play anyway. Alan Wheelis writes: "If . . . one's destiny is shaped from within then one has . . . gained freedom. This is self-transcendence. A process of change that originates in one's heart and expands outwards. . . . One gropes toward this vision in the dark, with no guide, no map and no guarantee. Here one acts as subject, author, creator. (Wheelis, 1979, p. 115)

The history of philosophy records the concurrent development of both idealism and humanism as perspectives of human behavior. In the fields of science and of psychotherapy idealistic philosophies are firmly established and humanistic concepts are regarded by scientific hardliners as unrealistic, unscientific, and unteachable. For those seeking to claim exclusive truth for one of these systems, the dichotomy between humanism and idealism presents an irreconcilable paradox (Chessick, 1977). I do not believe, however, that this paradox arises as the arcane product of an entrepreneurial elite seeking to succeed to gurudom, but is instead a faithful representation of the human psyche itself.

The existential view of human being is that the life history of the individual is formed by the imposition of meaning on the accident of experience. The problem of existential philosophy and therapy is: How is it possible for experience to have meaning? This is what existentialism calls the Question of Being. Until the last 200 years the mainstream of philosophical thought has not directed its attention to this question but has instead asked the question: What is the purpose of Being? In the effort to discover this purpose, philosophy has looked in two directions — outward to the tangible universe of nature and inward to the intangible universe of consciousness. The mission of idealistic philosophy is to discover an agent responsible for human experience and then to define its purpose.

History records the strategies man has developed to force this agent to reveal itself.

Primitive humans correctly divined that nature was the source of life and energy and they populated the worlds of nature and consciousness with benevolent and hostile forces according to their survival worth. Scientific man creates models which are tested by experiment. In the scientific universe, as in the occult world, nothing happens by chance. The properties of each electron, each particle of energy, are uniquely determined. Each particle has its own "space" and it must inexorably cooperate with every other particle of the universe. Nothing is out of place. Within the limits of the uncertainty principle, the space-energy of a particle can be followed through tremendous energy transformations. But it can never be said that this particle *experiences* anything. Indeed, in a universe where every state is choicelessly determined, experience has no meaning, whatever purpose the system may express.

Idealism, in its many forms, cannot, therefore, deal with the question: How is it possible for experience to have meaning? Its search for a transcendental agent of experience is mistaken. Human being is the agent of experience. There is no other. Experience only happens within human presence and only acquires meaning as a result of human choice. Consciousness is unique to the individual. One does not share it with other humans nor share it with universal particles. The existence of human consciousness may, indeed, be an expression of universal purpose; and consciousness may fruitfully speculate as to what that purpose might be. This book is not written either to advance or deter the cause of idealism. It attempts the modest enterprise of considering some of the ways by which individual experience acquires meaning regardless of what the ultimate purpose of human existence may be.

129

No one can evade the necessity for choosing a purpose for life. The trouble is not that individuals are trapped by the consequences of bad judgment. The trouble is that they have forgotten *how* they choose to understand their experience. Individuals are mentally and emotionally crippled not because they are unacquainted with approved social values or with the powers of the transcendent universe but because they have crippled their awareness of experience as well as their power to understand experience of which they could become aware. The legitimate focus of therapy is on these two issues. A therapy that bypasses these issues cannot liberate. The existential mission is not to discover the purpose of Being nor even to give it a meaning. It is to understand how choice leads to change.

Beyond considering the purpose of a process, there is also a difference between defining its dynamics and judging its results. Science in general, and scientific psychology in particular, devotes itself to studying processes of change. Natural science is not interested in the purposes of the universe nor in establishing social values. Its expertise lies in deriving rules of functioning. Behaviorism, as the most scientific effort of psychology, is not interested in defining values or expanding choices. It can train a rat to salute a flag but it has no concern for its sense of patriotism. Behaviorism seeks to increase predictability by limiting choices and degrading the meaning of experience. This is not necessarily a disadvantage. In the case of persons who suffer from memories of terrifying experiences, desensitization can be a beneficial treatment. In its emphasis on individual responsibility for evaluating experience, rather than conformity to dogmatic systems, science is humanistic. In its mission to discover a reality that is independent of human experience, science is idealistic. This dichotomy between humanism and idealism that can be found in every human endeavor reflects the dual nature of the psyche itself. These dual functions are, first, the apprehension of experience, and, second, the storing of judgments about the experience.

The self, as it is generally defined, is understood to be the accumulation of the object-images of experience. This is the personal self of the things one possesses: one's house, one's wife, one's job, one's feelings, etc. This is the self one is conscious *of*. It is available for evaluation and praise or criticism. "It" is an entity — an image — without consciousness of itself. "Its" do not have consciousness. They are only things to be conscious *of*. *Self*-consciousness is not a thing but a process — the process of discovering the power to create meaning. Words are necessary to communicate meaning, but *self*-consciousness — aware of choosing one's words, aware of choosing one's actions, aware of choosing one's feelings — means to-be. To-be is no referent for any thing. To-be has no *is*. To-be exis-ts. *Self*-consciousness is not some property added on to an entity as in "the sky is blue." *Self*-consciousness grounds human be-ing — unique, spontaneous, and undetermined. *Self*-consciousness is the subject, author, and creator of change that Wheelis has named. *Self*-consciousness is not a newcomer to the ken of psychology but has in the past been variously named "the individuated self," "the idealized self," "the transpersonal self," "the *I-am* ground of identity." Compared to ego, *self*-consciousness is a transcendent agent (May, 1958, p. 74), but not in the idealistic sense of another entity in a hall-of-mirrors game. It is the transcendent nature of human being itself. If the life-process of the psyche is the choice of meaning for apprehended events, *self*-consciousness is the recognition that *I* make that choice.

The life-mission of the individual is to find caring acceptance and validation from others and to protect one's self from physical and psychic injury. Authentic *self*hood is the actor in this complementary partnership with others. In the quest for *self*hood and the fulfillment of caring relationship, the secular therapist is an infant in the pantheon of spiritual explorers. The mission of recovering *self*-consciousness from unconscious concealment is not original to dynamic psychiatry.

It is the legacy of mythological antiquity. It has been through legend that the image and the promise of transcendent spiritual liberation have been transmitted. As innovative and revolutionary as we may believe the practice of secular therapy to be, we find ourselves but repeating the pattern of the ancient mysteries. The Astral Plane of antiquity has been recreated as the collective unconscious. The Secret Books of Wisdom have been restored with the authority of scientific theory and published as encyclopedias of psychiatric knowledge. And, as much as we may want to ignore it, hypnotic suggestion continues to claim a place as a method of therapeutic intervention.

The legacy of the journey to transcendent *self*hood has been transmitted from prehistory by the fairy tale. As Bettelheim (1977) has excellently detailed, the fairy tale embodies and is the guide to, the wisdom of aesthetic *self*hood. Bettelheim distinguished the fairy tale from the fable. The fairy tale presents no moral as does the fable. The fairy tale does not analyze or explain behavior. The witch is evil because she is a witch. The protagonists suffer because they are cursed. The characters do not introspect. They do not choose motives. They do not analyze relationships. They act their parts (not roles) because that is what they must do. Fairy tales have a purely existential goal. Their message is that human beings struggle through undeserved and unsolicited trials only in order to achieve their transcendent human nature. Fairy tales are ahistorical. They do not exemplify the evolution of human values or chronicle the solution of perplexing problems in social relationships. Problems are solved by living through them with the aide of intuitive hunches and with the aide of magic helpers—not by human passion or logical thought. The fairy tale, according to Bettelheim, teaches most effectively because it bypasses ego with its causal explanations of the world and directly contacts intuitive *self*-consciousness. This is also the task of the psychotherapist. The

132

skill of the psychotherapist lies in the ability to cast the facts of the client's situation into a story which conveys to the intuitive preconscious the goal of and the path to authentic *self*hood.

The sense of authentic *self*hood comes to us unchanged from the dawn of history. Bronowski (1973) points to the imprint of the artist's hand on the Ice Age cave paintings of 20,000 B.C. He envisions the artist to be saying to posterity, "This is my mark. This is man." This anticipates today's statement of existential *Dasein* — I am being here now. For those who can hold in awe this evidence of historic continuity of *self*-consciousness, the enterprise of psychotherapy is lifted out of the narrow context of scientific objectivity and restored to the path of transcendent spiritual destiny. This is not to discard the work of any who have labored to liberate the psyche from bondage to occult powers. In our day, however, there is need of a theory of human be-ing that can integrate the findings of scientific observation with the ancient quest for *self*-hood.

I believe the principles of existential philosophy can meet this need. The existential philosophers such as Kant, Kierkegaard, Marcel, Heidegger, and Jaspers are the modern-day exponents of the transcendent destiny of human being (Barrett, 1964). Writers in the field of anthropology such as Campbell (1949) and Frazer (1922), as well as therapists such as Kopp (1972), Naranjo (1972), and Van Dusen (1972), have also revalued the knowledge of the ancients. It may appear to be scientific sacrilege to those living in the world where God is absent (not dead) to equate religious mysticism with therapeutic liberation, but, to the client who comes for help, the words of Meister Eckhart — "But if it not take place in me, what avails it?" — speak more to his need than credentials of scientific enlightment. And for this *it* to take place in the client the therapist needs to be on the path with him.

133

The path of caring as a state of *self*-consciousness has been the immemorial concern of mystics, as Underhill has reported

(1961). She describes the mystical quest for a grasp of the meaning of Being and wonderfully anticipates the conclusions of existential philosophy. The mystical hunger for a sense of personal destiny and fulfillment of loving relationship bespeaks the need of each of us. Mendel (1976) recently identified prime human needs as the ability to manage anxiety, the capacity to form interpersonal relationships, and the possession of a sense of personal history. Failure to achieve a modicum of these qualities produces the familiar symptoms of exhaustion, depression, emptiness, hopelessness, and hostility. Every candidate for psychotherapy brings some of these symptoms to therapists for repair. Out of their background of training and experience therapists may provide educative counsel, emotional support and/or reconstructive therapy. Each therapist brings a unique background of experience to the meeting with the client. The purpose of this work is to show how therapists might approach their practice from an existential perspective.

The enterprise of existential psychotherapy is the recovery of *self*-consciousness from concealment in the unconscious. Individual *self*-consciousness is founded on the choice of the meaning of experience. The process of choosing this meaning is named Being-in-the-world (Heidegger, 1962).[5] I am the author and creator of this world. I acknowledge my responsibility for choosing the meaning of each situation that I engage my-*self* in. The name of this choosing is Care. Without Caring I cannot be my-*self* nor can I claim a personal world. The external objective world is only a meaningless succession of events until I Care to define its meaning for my-*self*. If I do not Care to make this choice I am a meaningless object for my-*self* regardless of what I may mean to others. My-*self* is born from consciousness of Caring and lives to Care for it-*self*. For my-*self* the choice of a meaning for my future death is the path to transcendent freedom. Now there is no other *I* to appeal to—past experience and future possibility belong to my-*self* alone. This is my personal history.

134

I am vulnerable to fear when I abandon Caring-to-be-in-the-world; and what I fear most is knowledge of this abandonment which I am unable to conceal from my-*self* by hiding in the everyday world of anonymity. Conscience calls my-*self* back from anonymity. The surrender to this call is freedom. *Self*-direction of my life is faith. To-be faithful is:

To step above [mental imagery] with great courage and with determination and with a devout and pleasant stirring of love, and . . . try to pierce that darkness which is above [me] . . . and to strike that thick cloud of unknowing with a sharp dart of longing love . . . and not retreat no matter what comes to pass. *The Cloud of Unknowing,* 14th Century. (Progoff, 1957, p. 73)

The capacity for scientific objectivity arises from the power of thinking to stand outside of appearances. But the knowledge attained in this manner is an illusion that prevents one from contacting the real world. To see this illusion for what it is brings one into the presence of a freedom of being that one will never be content to surrender.

EPILOGUE

PSYCHOTHERAPISTS
attempt to assist individuals who are searching for the good
life. However well- or ill-prepared they were, aesthetic enjoyment and ethical control have eluded them. Seemingly without power or knowledge, they present themselves to the therapist for his ministrations. Psychotherapy is a voyage of exploration through which the client discovers that the obstacles to
self-expression, which seemed so forbidding and impenetra-
ble and so necessary, are illusions of his or her own making.
The art of the therapist is to show the client the possibility of
exchanging the illusion of salvation through power and knowledge for the reality of caring human contact. When he does
this the client will find the wisdom to choose what he needs in
that moment. Jessie Taft understood this when she wrote

> In the single interview, if that is all I allow myself to count on, if
> I am willing to take that one hour in and for itself, there is no time

137

to hide behind material, no time to explore the past or future. I my-self am the remedy at this moment if there is any, and I can no longer escape my responsibility, not for the client but for myself and my role in the situation. (Robinson, 1962, p. 166)

NOTES

1. *being, to-be, be-ing*. The word *being* is commonly used either as a noun denoting an object entity or as a copulative verb connecting objects as equals, as in "he is human." In existential terms *being* refers specifically to the process of existing. In this book the forms to-be and be-ing are used to qualify the process of existing. Thus to-be should be read as *to — be* and be-ing as be *— ing*. The emphasis is on the action denoted by the *to* and the *ing*.
2. Reinhardt (1960) presents an account of the views of the Vienna Circle and in particular those of Igor Caruso, an early existential therapist. Ruitenbeck (1962) also presents a number of papers relating psychotherapy with existential philosophy.
3. Contributions of Boss and Binswanger to existential psychoanalysis are discussed by Needleman (1968).
4. A factually correct account of the revolution in modern physics is given by Gamow in *Thirty Years That Shook Physics* (1966).
5. Gelven's *Commentary on Heidegger's Being and Time* (1970) is a readable exposition of Heidegger's philosophy.

REFERENCES

Auden, W. *Kierkegaard*. New York: David McKay Co., Inc., 1952.

Barrett, W. *What is Existentialism?* New York: Grove Press, Inc., 1964.

Bellak, L., Hurvich, M., and Gediman, H. *Ego Functions in Schizophrenics, Neurotics and Normals*. New York: John Wiley and Sons, 1973.

Berne, E. *Transactional Analysis in Psychotherapy*. New York: Grove Press, Inc., 1961.

_____. *Games People Play*. New York: Grove Press, Inc., 1964.

_____. *What Do You Say After You Say Hello?* New York: Grove Press, Inc., 1972.

_____. *Beyond Games and Scripts*. C. Steiner and C. Kerr (Eds.) New York: Ballantine Books, 1976.

Bettelheim, B. *The Uses of Enchantment*. New York: Alfred A. Knopf, Inc., 1977.

Binswanger, L. "Freud and the Magna Carta of Clinical Psychology." In J. Needleman (Ed.) *Being in the World*. New York: Harper Torchbooks, 1968.

Brandon, D. *Zen in the Art of Helping*. London: Routledge and Kegan Paul, 1976.

141

Bronowski, J. *The Ascent of Man*. Boston: Little Brown and Co., 1973.

Buber, M. *I and Thou*. New York: Charles Scribner's Sons, 1958.

Campbell, J. *The Hero With a Thousand Faces*. Princeton, New Jersey: Princeton University Press, 1949.

Camus, A. *The Myth of Sisyphus*. New York: Alfred A. Knopf, Inc. 1955.

Capra, F. *The Tao of Physics*. New York: Bantam Books, Inc., 1977.

Chessick, R. "Effects of the Therapist's Philosophical Premises On The Psychotherapeutic Process." *American Journal of Psychotherapy*, 1977, *31*, 252-264.

Coan, R. *Hero, Artist, Sage or Saint*. New York: Columbia University Press, 1977.

Corsini, R. *Current Psychotherapies*. Itasca, Illinois: F. E. Peacock Publishers, Inc., 1979.

DeRopp, R. *The Master Game*. New York: Dell Publishing Co., Inc., 1968.

Edwards, D. "Waiting: An Existential Dynamic of Rackets." *Transactional Analysis Journal*, 1972, *2*, 89-90.

———. "The *Family* — A Therapeutic Model for the Treatment of Drug Addiction." *Clinical Social Work Journal*, 1973, *1*, 3-12.

———. "Counter-Transference Revisited in Marital Therapy." *The Marriage and Family Counselors Quarterly*, 1978, *12*, 32-36.

Ellis, A. "Rational Emotive Therapy." In R. Corsini (Ed.) *Current Psychotherapies*. Itasca, Illinois: F. E. Peacock Publishers, Inc., 1979.

Erickson, M., and Rossi, E. *Hypnotherapy, An Exploratory Casebook*. New York: Irvington Publishers, Inc., 1979.

Erikson, E. *Childhood and Society* (2nd ed.). New York: W. W. Norton and Co., Inc., 1963.

Fabry, J. *The Pursuit of Meaning*. Boston: Beacon Press, 1968.

Fagen, J., and Shepard, I. *Gestalt Therapy Now*. Palo Alto, California: Science and Behavior Books, Inc., 1970.

Frankl, V. *Man's Search for Meaning*. New York: Washington Square Press, 1963.

———. *Psychotherapy and Existentialism*. New York: Washington Square Press, 1967.

Frazer, J. *The Golden Bough*. New York: The Macmillan Co., 1922.

Gamow, G. *Thirty Years that Shook Physics*. New York: Anchor Books, 1966.

Gelven, M. *A Commentary on Heidegger's Being and Time*. New York: Harper and Row, 1970.

Gendlin, E. *Focusing*. New York: Everest House, 1978.

Glasser, W., and Zunin, L. "Reality Therapy." In R. Corsini (Ed.). *Current Psychotherapies*. Itasca, Illinois: F. E. Peacock Publishers, Inc. 1979.

Goulding, M. Private communication, 1980.

Goulding, M., and Goulding, R. *Changing Lives Through Redecision Therapy*. New York: Brunner/Mazel, Publishers, 1979.

Goulding, R., and Goulding, M. *The Power is in the Patient*. San Fransisco: T.A. Press, 1978.

Haley, J. *Uncommon Therapy: The Psychiatric Techniques of Milton H. Erickson, M. D.* New York: W. W. Norton and Co., Inc., 1973.

_____. *Strategies of Psychotherapy*. New York: Grune and Stratton, 1963.

Heidegger, M. "What is Metaphysics?" In W. Brock (Ed.) *Existence and Being*. Chicago, Illinois: Henry Regnery Company, 1949.

_____. *Being and Time*. New York: Harper and Row, 1962.

Hellman, L. *Pentimento*. Boston: Little Brown and Co., 1973.

Jaspers, K. *The Nature of Psychotherapy*. Chicago: University of Chicago Press, 1964.

Jung, C. "Aion: Phenomenology of the Self." In J. Campbell (Ed.) *The Portable Jung*. New York: The Viking Press, 1971.

Keleman, S. *Living Your Dying*. New York: Random House, 1974.

_____. *The Human Ground*. Palo Alto, California: Science and Behavior Books, 1975.

Kierkegaard, S. *The Present Age*. Princeton, New Jersey, Princeton University Press, 1940.

_____. *Fear and Trembling*. Princeton, New Jersey: Princeton University Press, 1941, a.

_____. *The Sickness Unto Death*. Princeton, New Jersey: Princeton University Press, 1941, b.

_____. *Concluding Unscientific Postscript*. Princeton, New Jersey: Princeton University Press, 1941, c.

_____. *The Concept of Dread*. Princeton, New Jersey: Princeton University Press, 1944,

Kohut, H. *The Analysis of the Self*. New York: International Universities Press, Inc., 1971.

———. *The Restoration of the Self*. New York: International Universities Press, Inc., 1977.

Kopp, S. *If You Meet the Buddha On the Road, Kill Him*. Palo Alto, California: Science and Behavior Books, 1972.

Koyre, A. *From the Closed World to the Infinite Universe*. New York: Harper Torchbooks, 1958.

Krill, D. *Existential Social Work*. New York: The Free Press, 1978.

Krishnamurti, J. *Talks and Dialogues*. New York: Avon Books, 1970.

Kübler-Ross, E. *On Death and Dying*. New York: Macmillan Publishing Co., Inc., 1969.

Laing, R. *The Divided Self*. New York: Pantheon Books, 1969, a.

———. *Self and Others*. New York: Pantheon Books, 1969, b.

Le Shan, L. "Physicists and Mystics: Similarities in World View." In *The Medium, The Mystic and the Physicist*. New York: Ballantine Books, 1974.

———. *How to Meditate*. New York: Bantam Books, 1975.

Lewis, H. *Shame and Guilt in Neurosis*. New York: International Universities Press, Inc., 1971.

Lichtenstein, H. "Some Considerations Regarding the Phenomenology of the Repetition Compulsion and the Death Instinct." *The Annual of Psychoanalysis* (Vol. II). New York: International Universities Press, 1975.

Luthe, W. *Autogenic Therapy* (Vol I). New York: Grune and Stratton, 1969.

Lynd, H. *On Shame and the Search for Identity*. New York: Harcourt Brace Jovanovich, Inc., 1958.

Masters, R., and Houston, J. *Mind Games*. New York: Dell Publishing Co., Inc. 1972.

May, R., Angel, E., and Ellenberger, H. *Existence*. New York: Basic Books, Inc., 1958.

Mendel, W. *Schizophrenia: The Experience and Its Treatments*. San Francisco: Jossey-Bass, Inc., 1976.

Menninger, K. *Man Against Himself*. New York: Harcourt Brace and World, Inc., 1938.

Naranjo, C. *The One Quest*. New York: The Viking Press, 1972.

———. *The Techniques of Gestalt Therapy*. Berkeley, California: The SAT Press, 1973.

Needleman, J. *Being in the World*. New York: Harper Torchbooks, 1968.

Niebuhr, R. *The Nature and Destiny of Man.* New York: Charles Scribner's Sons, 1949.

Perls, F. *Ego, Hunger and Aggression.* San Francisco: Orbit Graphic Arts, 1966.

_____. *Gestalt Therapy Verbatim.* Lafayette, California: Real People Press, 1969.

_____. *The Gestalt Approach and Eyewitness to Therapy.* Ben Lomond, California: Science and Behavior Books, 1973.

Perls, F., and Baumgartner, P. *Legacy from Fritz.* Palo Alto, California: Science and Behavior Books, Inc., 1975.

Perls, F. Hefferline, R., and Goodman, P. *Gestalt Therapy.* New York: Dell Publishing Co., Inc., 1951.

Piers, F., and Singer, M. *Shame and Guilt.* Springfield, Illinois: Charles C. Thomas, 1953.

Progoff, I. (Ed.) *The Cloud of Unknowing.* New York: The Julian Press, 1957.

Reich, W. *Character Analysis.* New York: Pocket Books, 1976.

Reinhardt, K. *The Existentialist Revolt.* New York: Frederick Ungar Publishing Co., 1960.

Robinson, V. (Ed.) *Jessie Taft, Therapist and Social Work Educator.* Philadelphia: University of Pennsylvania Press, 1962.

Rogers, C. "Client-Centered Therapy." In S. Arieti (Ed.) *American Handbook of Psychiatry.* (Vol. III). New York: Basic Books, Inc., 1966.

Ruitenbeck, H. (Ed.) *Psychoanalysis and Existential Philosophy.* New York: E. P. Dutton and Co., 1962.

Rychlak, J. *The Psychology of Rigorous Humanism.* New York: John Wiley and Sons, 1977.

Sahakian, W. *Psychotherapy and Counseling: Studies In Technique.* Chicago: Rand McNally, 1976.

Sartre, J.-P. *The Transcendence of the Ego.* New York: The Noonday Press, 1957.

_____. *The Philosophy of Jean-Paul Sartre.* R. Cumming (Ed.) New York: The Modern Library, 1965.

Satir, V. *Conjoint Family Therapy.* Palo Alto, California: Science and Behavior Books, Inc., 1964.

_____. *Peoplemaking.* Palo Alto, California: Science and Behavior Books, Inc., 1972.

Schiff, A., and Schiff, J. "Passivity." *Transactional Analysis Journal.* 1971, *1*, 71-78.

Schiff, J. *All My Children.* New York: Pyramid Books, 1972.

Schutz, W. " Encounter." In R. Corsini (Ed.), *Current Psychother-*

apies. Itasca, Illinois: F. E. Peacock Publishers, Inc., 1979.

Seguin, C. *Love and Psychotherapy*. New York: Libra Publishers, Inc., 1965.

Seligman, M. *Helplessness*. San Francisco: W. H. Freeman and Co., 1975.

————. "Coping with Stress." Presentation at the University of California Extension Division, San Francisco, California. November, 1979.

Selye, H. *The Stress of Life*. New York: McGraw Hill, 1976.

Shostrom, E. (Producer) *Three Approaches to Psychotherapy* (Film). Santa Ana, California: Psychological Films, Inc. 1965.

Simeons, A. *Man's Presumptuous Brain*. New York: E. P. Dutton and Co., 1962.

Simkin, J. *Mini Lectures in Gestalt Therapy*. Albany, California: Word Press, 1974.

Simon, S. "Synanon: Toward Building a Humanistic Organization." *Journal of Humanistic Psychology*. 1978, *18*, 3-20.

Speigel, J., and Bell, N. "The Family of the Psychiatric Patient." In S. Arieti (Ed.) *American Handbook of Psychiatry*. (Vol. I.) New York: Basic Books, Inc., 1959.

Stern, E. "Uses of Depression." Presentation at the American Academy of Psychotherapists Institute, Monterey, California, October 19, 1978.

Toffler, A. *Future Shock*. New York: Random House, 1970.

Toynbee, A. *A Study of History*. (Vol. VI). London, Oxford University Press, 1939.

Unamuno, M. *Tragic Sense of Life*. New York: Dover Publications, 1954.

Underhill, E. *Mysticism*. New York: E. P. Dutton and Co., Inc. 1961.

Van Dusen, W. *The Natural Depth in Man*. New York: Harper and Row, 1972.

Verdi, G. *Otello* (record). RCA Records, New York, NY.

Voices: Journal of the American Academy of Psychotherapists. 1978, *14*, No. 3.

Watzlawick, P. *How Real is Real?* New York: Random House, Inc. Publishers, 1978.

————. *The Language of Change*. New York: Basic Books, Inc. Publishers, 1978.

Watzlawick, P., Beavin, J. and Jackson, D. *Pragmatics of Human*

Communication. New York: W. W. Norton and Co., Inc. 1967.

Watzlawick, P., Weakland, J., and Fisch, R. *Change.* New York: W. W. Norton and Co., Inc., 1974.

Weil, S. *The Iliad or The Poem of Force.* Wallingford, Pennsylvania: Pendle Hill, 1956.

Weiss, D. *Existential Human Relations.* Montreal: Dawson College Press, 1975.

Wheelis, A. *The Desert.* New York: Basic Books, Inc., 1970.

Whitaker, C. "Psychotherapy of the Absurd: With Special Emphasis on the Psychotherapy of Aggression." *Family Process.* 1975, *14*, 1-16.

White, R. "Motivation Reconsidered: The Concept of Competence." *Psychological Review.* 1959, *66*, 297-333.

Yalom, I. *Existential Psychotherapy.* New York: Basic Books, Publishers, Inc. 1980.

INDEX

149

154